Nick Vandome

iPhone
for Seniors

for iPhone models with iOS 10

illustrated using iPhone 7 and iPhone 7 Plus

In easy steps is an imprint of In Easy Steps Limited
16 Hamilton Terrace · Holly Walk · Leamington Spa
Warwickshire · United Kingdom · CV32 4LY
www.ineasysteps.com

Notice of Liability
Every effort has been made to ensure that this book contains accurate
and current information. However, In Easy Steps Limited and the
author shall not be liable for any loss or damage suffered by readers
as a result of any information contained herein.

Trademarks
iPhone® is a registered trademark of Apple Computer, Inc. All other
trademarks are acknowledged as belonging to their respective
companies.

In Easy Steps Limited supports The Forest Stewardship Council (FSC),
the leading international forest certification organization. All our titles
that are printed on Greenpeace approved FSC certified paper carry the
FSC logo.

MIX
Paper from
responsible sources
FSC® C020837

Printed and bound in the United Kingdom

ISBN 978-1-84078-743-6

Contents

7   Hands on with Apps   115

8   Apps for Every Day   131

9   Relaxing with your iPhone   143

① Your New iPhone 7

The iPhone 7 is a sleek, stylish smartphone that is ideal for anyone, of any age. This chapter introduces the two models of the iPhone 7 and takes you through its buttons and controls. It also shows how to set it up ready for use and access some of its features and settings to get started.

Hands on with your iPhone

The iPhone is one of the great success stories of the digital age. It is the world's leading smartphone: a touchscreen phone that can be used for not only making calls and sending text messages, but also for online access and a huge range of tasks through the use of apps (programs that come pre-installed, or can be downloaded from the online Apple App Store). Essentially, the iPhone is a powerful, compact computer that can be used for communication, entertainment, organization and most things in between.

The latest iPhone is the iPhone 7 and it comes in two sizes: the iPhone 7, which has a screen size of 4.7 inches (measured diagonally) and the iPhone 7 Plus, which has a screen size of 5.5 inches (measured diagonally). Apart from their sizes, both models have the same features, functionality and operating system (iOS 10). Some of the features on the front of the iPhone 7 include:

'Apps' is just a fancy name for what are more traditionally called programs in the world of computing. See Chapter Seven for more information about apps.

Due to its larger screen size, the iPhone 7 Plus is capable of displaying the Home screen in both portrait and landscape mode. The iPhone 7 Plus also has a slightly superior iSight camera (on the back of the iPhone).

Front-facing camera (FaceTime)

Home screen

Apps, which give the iPhone its functionality

Dock, for storing frequently-used apps

The New icon pictured above indicates a new or enhanced feature introduced with the iPhone 7 or the latest version of its operating system, iOS 10.

Home button (can also serve as a Touch ID sensor)

What do you get?

The iPhone box contains all of the items required to use your new iPhone, charge it and open the SIM tray to add a SIM card. The various components are:

- **iPhone 7 or 7 Plus**. The iPhone will be turned off, but there should be enough charge in the battery to turn it on without having to charge it first. Press on this button to turn on the iPhone.

- **The Lightning to USB cable**. This can be used for charging the iPhone, or connecting it to a computer for downloading items.

- **The EarPods**. These can be used to listen to audio items on your iPhone. They can also be used to manage phone calls using the central control button (see page 52 for details). There is no headphone jack for the iPhone 7 EarPods, as they connect via the Lightning connector.

- **The Lightning to 3.5mm headphone jack adapter**. This can be used to connect headphones that have the traditional 3.5mm jack connection.

- **The SIM tool**. This is a small metal gadget that is in a cardboard envelope in the iPhone box. It is used to open the SIM tray so that a SIM card can be inserted (see pages 12-13 for details).

There is a wide range of accessories for the iPhone. These include cases in a range of colors and materials. These cases give some protection to the body of your iPhone.

To charge your iPhone with the Lightning to USB cable: insert the Lightning connector into the bottom of the iPhone, and insert the USB connector into the plug that is also provided in the iPhone box. Connect the plug to a socket to charge your iPhone.

iPhone Nuts and Bolts

For more details on turning on the iPhone, see page 15.

On/Off button

The button for turning the iPhone On and Off (and putting it into Sleep mode) is located on the top right-hand side of the body (looking at the screen). As with other buttons on the body, it is slightly raised, to make it easier to locate just by touch.

The iPhone 7 and 7 Plus come in Jet Black, Black, Silver, Gold and Rose Gold.

Volume controls

Volume is controlled using two separate buttons on the left-hand side of the body. They do not have symbols on them but they are used to increase and decrease the volume.

Ringer/silent (use this to turn the ringer on or off for when a call or a notification is received)

Volume up

Volume down

10

To make phone calls with your iPhone you need to have an active SIM card inserted and a suitable service provider for cellular (mobile) calls and data. The iPhone 7 uses a nano SIM card which is smaller than both the standard size and the micro size.

The Nano SIM Tray

The iPhone 7 uses a nano SIM (smaller than the micro SIM which is used in some older iPhone models).

Push the SIM tool firmly into this hole to access the SIM tray and insert a SIM card (see pages 12-13 for details)

Lightning connector, speakers and microphone
These are located at the bottom of the iPhone.

Stereo speakers

Microphone   Lightning connector

Back view of the iPhone 7
This contains the main camera, the LED flash and the rear microphone.

Rear microphone   LED flash (and torch)

iSight camera

The iPhone 7 Plus has two lenses for the iSight Camera, one wide-angle and one telephoto. They combine to take each shot.

Don't forget

The iSight camera is a high-quality 12 megapixel camera. It can capture excellent photos and also 4K (ultra-high definition) and high definition (HD) video. The iSight camera on the iPhone 7 Plus also comes with a wide-angle and telephoto lens capability. The front-facing FaceTime camera (see page 8) has a lower resolution (7 megapixels) and although it can also be used for photos and videos, it is best used for video calls using the FaceTime app (see pages 112-113). It can also be used for taking "selfies", the modern craze of taking a photo of yourself and then posting it online on a social media site such as Facebook.

Inserting the SIM

The SIM card for the iPhone 7 will be provided by your mobile carrier, i.e. the company that provides your cellular phone and data services. Without this, you would still be able to communicate with your iPhone, but only via Wi-Fi and compatible services. A SIM card gives you access to a mobile network too. Some iPhones come with the SIM pre-installed but you can also insert one yourself. To do this:

Don't forget

The phone services for the iPhone are provided by companies that enable access to their mobile networks, which you will be able to use for phone calls, texts and mobile data for access to the internet. Companies provide different packages: you can buy the iPhone for a reduced sum and then pay a monthly contract, typically for 12 or 24 months. Despite the fact that the iPhone will be cheaper, this works out more expensive over the period of the contract. Another option is to buy the iPhone (make sure it is unlocked so that you can use any SIM card) and use a SIM-only offer. This way you can buy a package that suits you for calls, texts and mobile data. Look for offers that have unlimited data for internet access.

1 Take the SIM tool out of the iPhone box and remove it from its cardboard packaging

2 Insert the SIM tool into the small hole next to the SIM slot on the side of the iPhone 7, as shown on page 10

3 Press the tool firmly into the hole so that the SIM tray pops out and starts to appear. Pull the SIM tray fully out

4 Place the SIM card with the metal contacts face downwards. Place the SIM tray in position so that the diagonal cut is in the same position as the cut on the SIM card

If you lose the SIM tool you can use the end of a stretched-out paper clip instead.

5 Place the SIM card into the SIM tray. It should fit flush, resting on a narrow ridge underneath it, with the diagonal cut on the card matching the cut in the tray

6 Place your thumb over the bottom of the SIM tray, covering the SIM card, and place the tray into the SIM slot, with the metal contacts facing the back of the phone. Push the tray firmly into the slot until it clicks into place

The SIM tray can only be inserted in one way. If it appears to encounter resistance, do not force it; take it out and try again. The hole in the SIM tray should be nearest to the bottom of the phone body.

13

Beware

The amount of storage you need may change once you have bought your iPhone. If possible, buy a version with as much storage as your budget allows.

Don't forget

3G and 4G refer to the data speeds for mobile connections. The G stands for Generation. 4G is faster than 3G and is becoming more widely available from mobile network providers.

Hot tip

To connect your iPhone to an HDTV you will need an Apple Lightning (or Dock) Digital AV Adapter or an Apple Lightning (or Dock) to VGA Adapter (sold separately).

iPhone Specifications

Apart from their sizes, the iPhone 7 and iPhone 7 Plus models have almost identical specifications:

- **Processor**: This determines the speed at which the iPhone 7 operates and how quickly tasks are performed. Both models have a fast A10 processor.

- **Screen**: The iPhone 7 has a 4.7 inch screen and for the iPhone 7 Plus it is 5.5 inches. Both are Retina HD quality which gives a very clear, sharp image.

- **Storage**: This determines how much content you can store on your iPhone. For the iPhone 7 and 7 Plus, the range of storage is either 32GB, 128GB, or 256GB.

- **Connectivity**: The options for this are Wi-Fi (support for fast 802.11ac Wi-Fi) and 3G/4G connectivity for calls and the internet, and Bluetooth 4.2 for connecting to devices over short distances.

- **Operating system**: Both the iPhone 7 and the iPhone 7 Plus run on the iOS 10 operating system.

- **Battery power**: The iPhone 7 provides up to 40 hours of wireless audio playback, 13 hours' video playback and 14 hours' talk time on 3G. The iPhone 7 Plus provides 60 hours for wireless audio, 14 for video and 21 hours' talk time. Web use over Wi-Fi is up to 12 and 13 hours respectively for the iPhone 7 and iPhone 7 Plus, with both slightly lower over 3G/4G.

- **Input/Output**: These are a Lightning connector port (for charging, headphones and connecting to a computer), built-in speaker and a built-in microphone (the iPhone 7 does not have a separate headphone jack).

- **Sensors**: The sensors in the iPhone 7 are: accelerometer, ambient light sensor and gyroscope.

- **TV and video**: This connects your iPhone to a High Definition TV with AirPlay Mirroring, which mirrors what's on your iPhone, wirelessly via Apple TV.

Turning On

The first thing you will want to do with your iPhone is to turn it on. To do this:

1 Press and hold on the **On/Off** button for a few seconds. Keep it pressed until the Apple icon appears

2 After a few seconds the iPhone will power on, displaying the Lock screen. Press the **Home** button to access the Home screen

If your iPhone ever freezes, or if something is not working properly, it can be rebooted by holding down the **Home** button and the **On/Off** button for 10 seconds and then turning it on again by pressing and holding the **On/Off** button.

Buy a glass screen protector to help preserve your iPhone's screen. This will help prevent marks and scratches and can also save the screen if it is broken: the protector breaks rather than the iPhone's screen itself.

Turning Off and Sleep

Whenever the iPhone is not in use it is a good idea to put it to sleep, or turn it off, to save power. If you will be using it again shortly then Sleep is the best option, but if you are not going to be using the phone for a longer period, e.g. overnight, then it may be best to turn it off.

To put the iPhone to sleep:

Don't forget

In Sleep mode (also known as Standby) the iPhone 7 will retain battery power for up to 10 days (240 hours). For the iPhone 7 Plus this is 16 days (384 hours).

1 Press the **On/Off** button once to put the iPhone to sleep and activate the Lock screen

To turn the iPhone off:

Don't forget

You will need an Apple ID for all Apple online services. This is free, and to register go to **https://appleid. apple.com**

Tap on **Create Your Apple ID**. You will be prompted to enter your email address and a password. Then follow the simple on-screen instructions including agreeing to their terms. Tap on Create Apple ID when ready.

1 Press and hold the **On/Off** button until the power off screen appears. Swipe the **slide to power off** button to the right to turn off the iPhone

Getting Set Up

When you first turn on your iPhone 7, there will initially be a series of Setup screens to move through before you can use the iPhone. These include the following options (a lot of these can be skipped during the Setup and accessed later from the **Settings** app):

- **Language**. Select the language you want to use.

- **Country**. Select the country in which you are located.

- **Location Services**. This determines whether your iPhone can use your geographical location for apps that use this type of information (such as Maps).

- **Wi-Fi network**. Select a Wi-Fi network to connect to the internet. If you are at home, this will be your own Wi-Fi network, if available. If you are at a Wi-Fi hotspot then this will appear on your network list.

- **Apple ID**. You can register with this to be able to access a range of Apple facilities, such as iCloud, FaceTime, Messages or to purchase items from the iTunes Store, the App Store or the iBooks Store. You can also create an Apple ID whenever you access one of the relevant apps for the first time.

- **iCloud**. This is Apple's online service for sharing and backing up content.

- **Find My iPhone**. This is a service that can be activated so that you can locate your iPhone if it is lost or stolen. This is done via the online iCloud site at **www.icloud.com**

- **Diagnostic information**. This enables information about your iPhone to be sent to Apple.

- **Start using**. Once the Setup process has been completed you can start using your iPhone.

The iPhone offers several features for users who have difficulty with hearing, vision, physical or motor skills. These are covered on pages 178-181.

For more information about using iCloud see Chapter Three.

The Find My iPhone function can also be set up within the **iCloud** section of the **Settings** app (see pages 184-185).

iPhone Settings

The Settings app is the one that should probably be explored first as it controls settings for the appearance of the iPhone and the way it, and its apps, operate. To use the Settings app:

1 Tap once on an item within the Settings app to see its options

The System Settings include:

- **Airplane Mode**. This can be used to disable network connectivity while on an airplane.

- **Wi-Fi**. This enables you to select a wireless network.

- **Bluetooth**. Turn this On to connect Bluetooth devices.

- **Cellular (Mobile Data)**. These are the settings that will be used with your cellular (mobile) service provider.

- **Personal Hotspot**. This can be used to share your internet connection.

- **Carrier**. This can be used to locate relevant signals from cellular carriers. By default it is On for Automatic.

- **Notifications**. This determines how the Notification Center operates (see pages 26-27).

- **Control Center**. This determines how the Control Center operates (see pages 34-35).

- **Do Not Disturb**. Use this to specify times when you do not want to receive audio alerts or FaceTime video calls.

- **General**. This contains a range of common settings.

- **Display & Brightness**. This can be used to set the screen brightness, text size and bold text.

- **Wallpaper**. This can be used to select a wallpaper.

- **Sounds**. This has options for setting sounds for alerts.

To change the iPhone's wallpaper, tap once on the **Choose a New Wallpaper** option in the **Wallpaper** setting. From here, you can select system images, or ones that you have taken yourself and saved on your iPhone.

18

...cont'd

- **Siri**. Options for using the digital voice assistant.

- **Touch ID & Passcode**. This has options for adding a passcode or fingerprint ID for unlocking the iPhone.

- **Battery**. This can be used to view battery usage by apps.

- **Privacy**. This can be used to activate Location Services so that your location can be used by specific apps.

- **iCloud**. This contains settings for items saved to iCloud.

- **iTunes & App Store**. This can be used to specify downloading options for the iTunes and App Stores.

- **Wallet & Apple Pay**. This can be used to add credit or debit cards for use with Apple Pay (see pages 42-45).

- **Mail, Contacts, Calendars**. These are three separate settings that have options for how these apps operate.

- **Notes**. This has formatting options for the Notes app.

- **Reminders**. This has an option for syncing your reminders for other devices, covering a period of time.

- **Phone**. Settings for making calls (see pages 68-69).

- **Messages**. Options for how the Messages app operates.

- **FaceTime**. This is used to turn video calling On or Off.

- **Maps**. This contains options for displaying distances and the default method for displaying map type.

- **Compass**. One setting, to use True North or not.

- **Safari**. Settings for the default iPhone web browser.

- **News**. Settings for specifying access for the News app.

- **Photos & Camera**. This has options for viewing and sharing photos using iCloud (see page 169).

- **Music, Videos, iBooks**, and **Podcasts**. Settings for how these four apps manage and display their content.

If a Settings option has an On/Off button next to it, this can be changed by swiping the button to either the left or right. Green indicates that the option is **On**. Select **Settings** > **General** > **Accessibility** > **On/Off Labels** to show or hide the icons on each button.

19

Tap on a link to see additional options:

Tap once here to move back to the previous page for the selected setting:

iPhone Sounds

Like all smartphones, the iPhone 7 comes with a variety of sound options, to identify different items such as calls, emails, texts and many more. You can customize these sounds, or turn them off for certain items.

Don't forget

If the Ringer button on the side of the iPhone is turned Off, the iPhone can still be set to vibrate if a call or notification is received, using the **Vibrate on Silent** button in Step 3.

1 Tap once on the **Settings** app

2 Tap once on the **Sounds** tab

3 In the **Vibrate** section, drag the two buttons

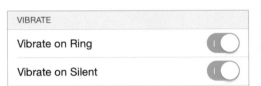

to **On** if you want the phone to vibrate when you receive a call and also when in silent mode

4 Drag this slider to change the volume of the ringer for when you receive a call or an alert sound

5 In the **Sounds and Vibration Patterns** section, tap once on an item for which you want to set an

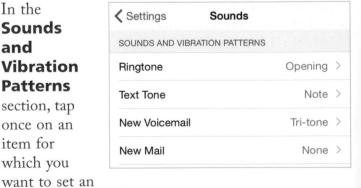

alert sound. This sound will be played whenever you receive one of these items, e.g. a new email

6 Tap once on the **Vibration** button

‹ Sounds	**New Mail**	Store
Vibration		None ›

7 Tap once on a vibration effect to use for the selected item. Tap once on the **New Mail** button to go back

‹ New Mail	**Vibration**	
STANDARD		
Accent		
Alert		
Heartbeat		

8 In the **Alert Tones** section tap once on an alert sound. A preview of the sound will be played. If you want to keep this alert sound, tap once on the **Sounds** button

‹ Sounds	**New Mail**	Store
Vibration		None ›
ALERT TONES		
✓ None		
Aurora		
Bamboo		
Chord		
Circles		

Store

21

9 In the main **Sounds** window, swipe to the

Keyboard Clicks	⬤
Lock Sounds	⬤

bottom of the window. Drag the buttons **On** or **Off** for a sound for when the screen is locked, and also for keyboard clicks when you type with the keyboard

About iOS 10

iOS 10 is the latest version of the operating system for Apple's mobile devices, including the iPhone and also the iPad and the iPod Touch.

iOS 10 further enhances the user experience for which the mobile operating system is renowned. This includes:

iOS 10 can only be installed on the iPhone 5 and later models. It comes pre-installed on the iPhone 7 and 7 Plus.

The Raise to Wake function can be turned **On** or **Off** within **Settings** > **Display & Brightness**.

- An enhanced Messages app for sending text messages. This now includes options for creating handwritten messages, adding quick replies (Tapback), customizing the way that message bubbles appear, enhanced options for adding emojis and even sending invisible messages.

- A revamped Photos app, including an improved search facility for finding photos, and also a Memories function which automatically collates the best photos from a time or location and even creates a movie of the photos.

- Raise to Wake. This is a function whereby the iPhone wakes from Sleep mode simply by lifting it up. The Lock screen is still activated, but notifications can be viewed so you can quickly see if you have received any text messages, emails or other notifications.

- A new version of the Lock screen that can be unlocked with the Home button, and also includes widgets that display real-time information about a range of items including the weather, news and the stock market. The Lock screen can also be used to display Notifications from different apps.

- An updated Control Center with additional controls, and a Night Shift mode that automatically adjusts the color of the display at night.

- Redesigned versions of the News and Music apps to create a more attractive layout and visual display.

- A new Home app that can be used to control compatible devices in your home, such as heating controls or turn lights on or off.

To check the version of the iOS, look in **Settings** > **General** > **Software Update**.

Using the Lock Screen

To save power it is possible to set your iPhone screen to auto-lock. This is the equivalent of the Sleep option on a traditional computer. To do this:

1 Tap once on the **Settings** app

2 Tap once on the **Display & Brightness** tab

AA Display & Brightness

3 Tap once on the **Auto-Lock** link

Auto-Lock   Never >

4 Tap once on the time of non-use after which you wish the screen to be locked

< Display & Brightness **Auto-Lock**

30 Seconds	
1 Minute	✓
2 Minutes	
3 Minutes	
4 Minutes	
5 Minutes	
Never	

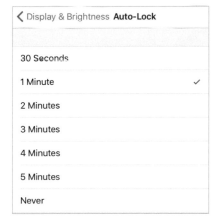

●●●○○ EE 🔒   🔋 80%

10:26
Friday, October 14

Press home to unlock

5 Once the screen is locked, press the **Home** button to unlock the screen

Don't forget

The screen can also be locked by pressing once on the **On/Off** button on the right-hand side of the iPhone's body.

Don't forget

Auto-locking the screen does not prevent other people from accessing your iPhone. If you want to prevent anyone else having access, it can be locked with a passcode or the Touch ID function. See pages 24-25 for details.

Hot tip

Swipe from right to left on the Lock screen to access the camera.

23

Touch ID and Passcode

Adding a passcode

When the iPhone is locked, i.e. the Lock screen is displayed, it can be unlocked simply by pressing the **Home** button. However, this is not secure, as anyone could unlock the phone. A more secure option is to add a numerical passcode. To do this:

Beware

If you use a passcode to lock your iPhone, write it down, but store it in a location away from the iPhone.

1 Select **Settings > Touch ID & Passcode**

2 Tap once on the **Turn Passcode On** button

Don't forget

Tap once on the **Passcode Options** link in Step 3 to access other options for creating a passcode. These include a **Custom Alphanumeric Code**, a **Custom Numeric Code** and a **4-Digit Code**. The 4-Digit Code is the least secure and the Alphanumeric Code is the most secure as it can use a combination of numbers, letters and symbols.

3 Enter a six-digit passcode. This can be used to unlock your iPhone from the Lock screen

4 Tap once on

the **Require Passcode** button in Step 2 to specify a time period until the passcode is required on the Lock screen. The best option is **Immediately**, otherwise someone else could access your iPhone

...cont'd

Fingerprint sensor with Touch ID

For greater security, the **Home** button can be used as
a fingerprint sensor to unlock your iPhone with the
fingerprint which has set it up. (A passcode also has to be
set up in case the Touch ID does not work.) To do this:

1 Select **Settings > Touch ID & Passcode**

2 Create a passcode as shown on the previous
page (this is required if the fingerprint sensor is
unavailable for any reason)

3 Drag the **iPhone
Unlock** button to **On**
and tap once on the
Add a Fingerprint...
link. This presents a
screen for creating your
Touch ID

4 Place your finger on the
Home button several
times until the Touch
ID is created. This will
include capturing the
edges of your finger.
The screens move
automatically after each
part is captured and the
fingerprint icon turns red

Hot tip

Touch ID can also be
used for contactless
purchases for Apple
Pay (see pages 42-45)
and purchases in the
iTunes and App Stores.
Drag the buttons **On**
in Step 3 if you want
to use these functions.
If these are activated
then purchases can be
made by pressing the
Home button with
your unique Touch ID.

Don't forget

The fingerprint sensor
is very effective,
although it may take
a bit of practice until
you can get the right
position for your
finger to unlock the
iPhone, first time,
every time. It can
only be unlocked
with the same finger
that created the
Touch ID in Step 4,
although more than
one fingerprint can be
added.

25

The Notification Center can be accessed by dragging down from the top of the screen, in any app.

Drag the **Show on Lock Screen** to **On** in Step 4 to enable notifications for the selected app to be displayed even when the iPhone is locked.

Text messages can be replied to directly from the Lock screen, without unlocking the iPhone. To do this, press on the message on the Lock screen and compose a reply as normal.

Notifications

Notifications can be used with iOS 10 so that you never miss an important message or update. Notifications can be viewed in the Notification Center and also on the Lock screen. To set up and use Notifications:

1 Tap once on the **Settings** app

2 Tap once on the **Notifications** tab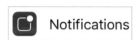

3 Under **Notification Style** tap once on an item to select the notification settings for a specific app

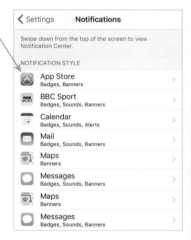

4 Drag the **Allow Notifications** button to **On** to display notifications from this app in the Notification Center

5 Tap here to select the style for how the notification appears

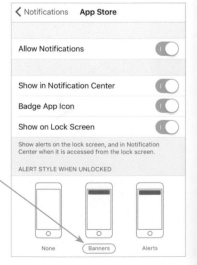

6 Swipe down from the top of the iPhone screen, from the Home screen or any app, to view your notifications in the Notification Center (if the Notification Center is accessed from within another app, the background is gray). This is split into two sections: the Today section which contains widgets with real-time information about topics such as the weather, stocks and news. It also contains the Up Next calendar item. Swipe to the left to view the other section, which contains notifications from the apps selected in Step 3 on the previous page

Tap on the small circle at the bottom of the Notification Center to move between the two pages.

7 Swipe to the bottom of the Today screen and tap once on the **Edit** button to manage the widgets that appear here. Tap on a red circle to delete a widget from the Today page or scroll down and tap on a green button to add a new widget

The Notification Center Today page can also be accessed by swiping from left to right on the main Home screen. Both pages can also be accessed by swiping down from the top of the Lock screen.

Updating Software

The operating system that powers the iPhone is known as iOS. This is a mobile computing operating system, and it is also used on the iPad and the iPod Touch. The latest version is iOS 10. Periodically, there are updates to the iOS to fix bugs and add new features. These can be downloaded to your iPhone once they are released:

28

1. Tap once on the **Settings** app. (A red tag indicates that an update is available)

2. Tap once on the **General** tab

3. Tap once on the **Software Update** link

4. If there is an update available it will be displayed here, with details of what is contained within it

5. Tap once here to start the downloading process. The iOS update will then be done automatically

2 Starting to use your iPhone 7

This chapter covers the functions on the iPhone that you need to use it confidently and make the most of its features. From working with apps to using Apple Pay to pay for items with your iPhone, it explains the iPhone environment so you can quickly get up and running with it.

Home Button

The **Home** button, located at the bottom-middle of the iPhone, can be used to perform a number of tasks:

1 Click once on the **Home** button to return to the Home screen at any point

The **Home** button can also be used as a fingerprint sensor to set up Touch ID for unlocking the iPhone. See pages 24-25 for details.

2 Double-click on the **Home** button to access the **App Switcher** window. This shows the most recently-used and open apps

Siri has to be turned **On** in **Settings** > **Siri** before it can be used.

3 Press and hold on the **Home** button to access the Siri voice assistant function (see pages 46-49)

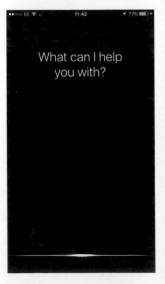

Opening and Closing Items

All apps on your iPhone can be opened with the minimum of fuss and effort:

1 Tap once on an icon to open the app

2 The app opens at its Home screen

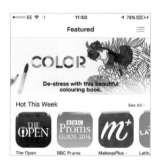

3 Click once on the **Home** button to return to the iPhone Home screen

4 From the App Switcher window (see previous page) swipe left and right between open apps and tap on one to make it the active app. Swipe an app to the top of the window in the App Switcher to close it

When you switch from one app to another, the first one stays open in the background. You can go back to it by accessing it from the App Switcher window or the Home screen.

To reopen an app that has been closed, click once on the **Home** button to go back to the Home screen and tap once on the app's icon here.

Using the Dock

By default, there are four apps on the Dock at the bottom of the iPhone's screen. These are the four that Apple thinks you will use most frequently:

- **Phone**, for making and receiving calls.
- **Safari**, for web browsing.
- **Messages**, for text messaging.
- **Music**.

With iOS 10, some of the pre-installed apps can be deleted from your iPhone. These are indicated by a cross in the top, left-hand, corner when you press on an app, as in Step 1.

You can rearrange the order in which the Dock apps appear:

1 Press and hold on one of the Dock apps until it starts to jiggle

Just above the Dock is a line of small white dots. These indicate how many screens of content there are on the iPhone. Tap on one of the dots to go to that screen.

2 Drag the app into its new position

3 Click once on the **Home** button to return from edit mode

Adding and removing Dock apps

You can also remove apps from the Dock and add new ones:

1 To remove an app from the Dock, press and hold it and drag it onto the main screen area

2 To add an app to the Dock, press and hold it and drag it onto the Dock

3 The number of items that can be added to the Dock is restricted to a maximum of four, as the icons do not resize

4 Click once on the **Home** button to return from edit mode

Don't forget

If items are removed from the Dock they are still available in the same way from the main screen. (When the iPhone 7 Plus is using landscape mode, the Dock appears down the right-hand side of the screen.)

Using the Control Center

The Control Center is a panel containing some of the most commonly-used options within the **Settings** app.

Accessing the Control Center

The Control Center can be accessed with one swipe from any screen within iOS 10 and it can also be accessed from the Lock screen. To set this up:

The Control Center cannot be disabled from being accessed from the Home screen.

1   Tap once on the **Settings** app

2   Tap once on the **Control Center** tab and drag the **Access on Lock Screen** and **Access Within Apps** buttons On or Off to specify if the Control Center can be accessed from there (if both are Off, it can still be accessed from any Home screen)

The Control Center also has an option for managing AirDrop, which is the functionality for sharing items wirelessly between compatible devices. Tap once on the **AirDrop** button in the Control Center and specify whether you want to share with **Contacts Only** or **Everyone**. Once AirDrop is set up, you can use the **Share** button in compatible apps to share items, such as photos, with any other AirDrop users in the vicinity.

3   Swipe up from the bottom of any screen to access the Control Center panel. Swipe from right to left to access the music player controls panel. Swipe down anywhere on the Control Center to close it

4   Use this slider to control the screen brightness

34

Control Center controls

The items that can be used in the Control Center are:

- Tap on this button to activate Night Shift mode. This can be used to adjust the phone's brightness at night time. This can also be changed in **Settings** > **Display & Brightness**.

- Tap once on this button to turn **Airplane mode** On or Off.

- Tap once on this button to turn **Wi-Fi** On or Off.

- Tap once on this button to turn **Bluetooth** On or Off.

- Tap once on this button to turn **Do Not Disturb** mode On or Off.

- Tap once on this button to **Lock** or **Unlock** screen rotation.

- Tap once on this button to access the **Torch**.

- Tap once on this button to access a **Clock**, including a stopwatch.

- Tap once on this button to access the **Calculator**.

- Tap once on this button to open the **Camera** app.

Bluetooth can be used to connect to other compatible devices, using radio waves over short distances up to approximately 20 meters. Both devices must have Bluetooth turned on and be 'paired' with each other. This links them together so that content, such as photos, can be shared between them.

If the screen rotation is **Locked**, the screen will not change orientation when the iPhone is moved.

Navigating Around

The iPhone screen is very receptive to touch and this is the main method of navigating around, through a combination of swiping, tapping and pinching.

Swiping between screens

Once you have added more apps to your iPhone they will start to fill up more screens. To move between these:

1 Swipe left or right with one or two fingers

You can also move between different screens by tapping once on the small white dots in the middle of the screen above the Dock.

You can also return to the first Home screen by clicking once on the **Home** button.

In addition to swiping between two screens there are a combination of tapping, swiping and pinching gestures that can be used to view items such as web pages, photos, maps and documents and also navigate around the iPhone.

Swiping up and down

Swipe up and down with one finger to move up or down web pages, photos, maps or documents. The content moves in the opposite direction of the swipe, i.e. if you swipe up, the page will move down and vice versa.

Tapping and zooming

Double-tap with one finger to zoom in on a web page, photo, map or document. Double-tap with one finger to return to the original view.

Pinching and swiping

Swipe outwards with thumb and forefinger to zoom in on a web page, photo, map or document.

The faster you swipe on the screen, the faster the screen moves up or down.

Swiping outwards with thumb and forefinger enables you to zoom in on an item to a greater degree than double-tapping with one finger.

Pinch together with thumb and forefinger to zoom back out on a web page, photo, map or document.

Reachability

Because of the size of both the iPhone 7 and iPhone 7 Plus, it is not always easy to access all items with one hand. This is overcome by a feature known as Reachability. This moves the items on the screen to the bottom half and they can all be accessed from here.

The Reachability feature can be accessed from any screen of the iPhone.

38

1 By default, all items on the screen take up the whole area

2 Gently double-tap on the **Home** button (this is not the same as double-clicking the **Home** button, which activates the App Switcher screen)

3 The items on the screen are minimized to the bottom half

4 The Reachability effect stays in place for one action, e.g. after you tap on an item the screen reverts to normal size

Zooming the Display

If you want the items on the iPhone 7 screen to be larger, this can be done with the Display Zoom feature. To do this:

1 Tap once on the **Settings** app

2 Tap once on the **Display & Brightness** tab

3 Tap once on the **View** button underneath **Display Zoom**

4 Tap once on the **Standard** button to view the current settings. Tap once on the **Zoomed** button to see the increased size

5 Tap once on the **Set** button to change the size of the items on the screen, then tap the **Zoomed** button to apply the change

The **Display & Brightness** settings can also be used to increase the text size for supported apps. Tap once on the **Text Size** button to access a slider with which you can set the required text size.

Using 3D Touch

One of the features using touch on the iPhone 7 is 3D Touch. This can be used to activate different options for certain apps, depending on the strength with which you press on an item. For instance, a single press, or tap, can be used to open an app. However, if you press harder on the app then different options appear. This can be used for Quick Actions, and Peek and Pop.

Quick Actions

These are some of the Quick Actions that can be accessed with 3D Touch:

Hot tip

Accessing the 3D Touch features requires specific extra pressure: it is not just a case of pressing with the same amount of pressure for a longer time. This is known as pressing 'deeper' into an app. This also provides a slight buzzing vibration, known as haptic feedback.

Don't forget

Most apps that have 3D Touch Quick Actions functionality are the pre-installed Apple ones. An increasing number of third-party apps also now support this, most notably social media apps such as Facebook and Twitter. Experiment by pressing deeper on different apps to see if they have options for 3D Touch.

1 Press deeper into the **Camera** app to access options for taking a selfie or recording a video, a slo-mo shot or a regular photo

2 Press deeper into the **Messages** app to access options for sending a text message to recent contacts or create a new message

3 Press deeper into the **Mail** app to access options for adding a VIP, creating a new email, searching for an email, accessing your VIP email contacts or accessing your Inbox

Peek and Pop

3D Touch can also be used to view items within apps, with a single press. This is known as Peek and Pop. To use this, with the Mail app:

1 Press on an email in your Inbox to peek at it, i.e. view it with the other items blurred out

Other apps that offer Peek and Pop include: Safari, Maps, Camera and Photos. Items for Safari and Maps can be peeked at and accessed from within an email, e.g. if there is a website link in an email, press it once to view a preview of the web page and press deeper to open it in Safari. Photos can be peeked at from the Camera app by pressing on a thumbnail image and then pressing deeper to open it.

2 Press deeper on the email to pop it open, i.e. view it in Preview mode, rather than opening it fully. (Swipe up on the Preview screen to access a menu for options for the email, e.g. Reply etc.)

3 Press deeper again on the email to open it fully in the Mail app and access its full functionality

41

About Apple Pay

Apple Pay is Apple's service for mobile, contactless, payment. It can be used by adding credit, debit and store cards to your iPhone 7, via the Wallet app, and then paying for items by using your Touch ID fingerprint as authorization for payment. Credit, debit and store cards have to be issued by banks or retailers who support Apple Pay, but there are an increasing number that do so, with more joining on a regular basis. Outlets also have to support Apple Pay but this, too, is increasing and, given the success of the iPhone, is likely to grow at a steady rate.

Setting up Apple Pay

To use Apple Pay you have to first add your cards to your iPhone 7 (and be signed in to iCloud):

Don't forget

At the time of printing, Apple Pay has no limit for in-store purchases in the US, but there are restrictions in other countries (e.g. maximum £30 in the UK). Visit **https://support.apple.com/en-us/HT201469** for further information.

Hot tip

Cards can also be added to the Wallet at any time from **Settings** > **Wallet & Apple Pay** > **Add Credit or Debit Card**.

Don't forget

If your bank does not yet support Apple Pay then you will not be able to add your credit or debit card details into the Wallet app.

1 Tap once on the **Wallet** app

2 Tap once on the **Add Credit or Debit Card** link or tap once on this button

Pay with Touch ID using Apple Pay. Make purchases in stores and in apps without swiping your card or entering your card and shipping details.

Add Credit or Debit Card

3 Tap once on the **Next** button

4 The card details can be added to the Wallet by taking a photo of the card. Place the card on a flat surface and position it within the white box. The card number is then added automatically. Alternatively, tap once on the **Enter Card Details Manually** link

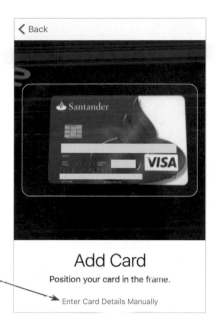

< Back

Add Card
Position your card in the frame.

Enter Card Details Manually

Beware

Obtaining your card number using the camera is not always completely accurate. Take the photo in good light, always check the number afterwards and amend it if necessary.

5 Tap once on the **Next** button to verify your card details (ensure the name is exactly the same as appears on the card)

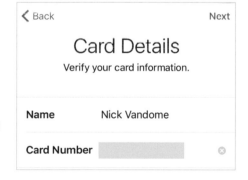

< Back   **Next**

Card Details
Verify your card information.

Name   Nick Vandome

Card Number

Don't forget

During the setup process you will also have to **Agree** to the Apple Pay Terms and Conditions.

Terms and Conditions
I agree to the Terms and Conditions.

Cancel	Agree

6 Add any additional details for the card (such as expiration date and the security code) and tap once on the **Next** button

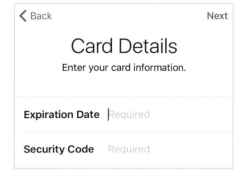

< Back   **Next**

Card Details
Enter your card information.

Expiration Date Required

Security Code   Required

43

...cont'd

Don't forget

Although no form of contactless payment is 100% secure, Apple Pay does offer some security safeguards. One is that no card information is passed between the retailer and the user: the transaction is done by sending an encrypted token that is used to authorize the payment. Also, the use of the Touch ID fingerprint ensures another step of authorization that is not available with all other forms of contactless payment.

Don't forget

You will be sent a text message or email confirming verification.

Don't forget

Numerous cards can be added within the Wallet app.

7 Before you can use Apple Pay, your bank or store card issuer has to verify your card. This can be done either by a text message or a phone call. Select the preferred method and tap once on the **Next** button

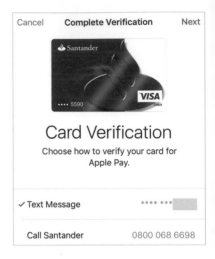

8 If you selected to verify your card with a text message above, you will be sent a code to verify your card. Enter this and tap once on the **Next** button. Once this has been done, the card will be activated. Tap once on the **Done** button on the Card Activated screen

9 Details of the card that has been added to the Wallet are displayed. This will be visible when you open the Wallet app, ready for use with Apple Pay

Using Apple Pay

Once credit, debit and store cards have been added to the Wallet app and authorized by the issuer, they can be used with Apple Pay in participating outlets. To do this:

1 When you go to pay for an item, open the **Wallet** app and tap once on the card you want to use. Hold your iPhone 7 up to the contactless payment card reader

2 Press the **Home** button to authorize the payment with Touch ID using your unique fingerprint. (Retailers must have a contactless card reader in order for Apple Pay to be used.) The payment should be processed

3 To view your payments, tap once on the Wallet app and select a card. The latest transaction is displayed, but not specific items that you have bought. This information is only visible to you and is not shared with Apple. Select **Settings > Wallet & Apple Pay** to view a longer list of transactions

Cards for Apple Pay can be accessed directly from the Lock screen, if this has been set up: **Settings > Wallet & Apple Pay** and turn On **Double-Click Home Button** under **Allow Access When Locked**.

Apple Pay can also be used on some online sites, in which case the Apple Pay logo will be displayed.

The Wallet app can also be used to scan or download items such as boarding passes and cinema tickets, and then used from the Lock screen. However, this can only be done with participating organizations.

Using Siri

Siri is the iPhone voice assistant that provides answers to a variety of verbal questions by looking at your iPhone and also web services. You can ask Siri questions relating to the apps on your iPhone, and also general questions such as weather conditions around the world, or sports results. Initially, Siri can be set up within the **Settings** app:

1 Tap once on the **Settings** app

2 Tap once on the **Siri** tab

Options for Siri
Within the Siri setting there are options for its operation:

1 Drag this button to **On** to enable Siri

2 Drag the **Allow "Hey Siri"** button to **On** if you want to be able to access Siri just by saying **Hey Siri**

3 Make selections here for the language, voice type, feedback and your own details to use with Siri

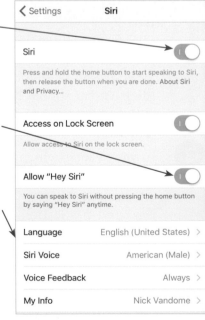

4 If using Hey Siri, it has to be set up by training it for your voice. Tap once on the **Set Up Now** button

> Cancel
>
> Set Up "Hey Siri"
>
> This helps Siri recognize your voice when you say "Hey Siri."
>
> Set Up Now

5 Repeat the range of phrases to train Siri to your voice. This is a five-step process

> Cancel   1 of 5
>
> Say "Hey Siri" into the iPhone

6 Tap once on the **Done** button to complete the Hey Siri setup

> Cancel
>
> "Hey Siri" Is Ready
>
> Siri will recognize your voice whenever you say, "Hey Siri."
>
> Done

Accessing Siri

There are two ways to access Siri (in addition to Hey Siri):

1 Press and hold the **Home** button until the Siri screen appears

What can I help you with?

Siri can be used to open any of the pre-installed iPhone apps, simply by saying, for example, **Open Photos**.

2 Ask your question to Siri. After the reply, tap once on the microphone button to ask another question

47

Finding Things with Siri

Siri is very versatile and can be used for a wide range of functions, including finding things on your iPhone, searching the web, getting weather forecasts, finding locations and even playing music.

Accessing your apps

To use Siri to find things on your iPhone:

Hot tip

Siri can also display specific contacts. Say, **Show me...** followed by the person's name to view their details (if they are in your contacts).

Hot tip

Siri can also read out your information: open an item such as calendar appointments and then say, **Read appointment**.

Don't forget

You can ask for weather forecasts for specific periods, such as **Today** or **This Week**. However, Siri's power of forecasting only stretches to 10 days in the future.

1 Access Siri as shown on page 47

2 To find something from your iPhone apps, ask a question such as, **Open my contacts**

3 The requested app is displayed

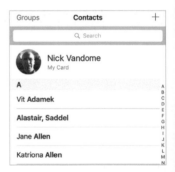

Getting the weather

You can ask Siri for weather forecasts for locations around the world. Simply ask for the weather in a certain city or location.

Finding locations

Siri is also effective for viewing locations within the Maps app. This can be done on an international, national or city level. Siri can also be used to get directions.

Siri in iOS 10 can be used with certain third-party apps to perform tasks such as booking a taxi or a restaurant table.

Searching locally

If Location Services is turned on for Siri, then you can ask for local information, such as, **Show the nearest Indian restaurants**.

Playing music

You can use Siri to play any of the music that you have in the Music app. Simply ask Siri to play a track and it will start playing. (Music can be downloaded from the iTunes Store app; see page 146 for more details).

Siri can also play a whole album as well as individual tracks. Ask for the album name to be played and Siri should oblige.

To stop a song, simply say **Stop playing** and the song will be paused.

Searching with Spotlight

Siri can be used to search for items on your iPhone, and you can also use the built-in text search engine, Spotlight. This can search over numerous items on your iPhone, and these can be selected within Settings:

Spotlight settings

Within the Settings app you can select which items the Spotlight search operates over. To do this:

To return to the Home screen from the Spotlight Search page, press once on the **Home** button.

1 Tap once on the **Settings** app

2 Tap once on the **General** tab

3 Tap once on the **Spotlight Search** link

Spotlight Search

4 Drag the green button to **Off** to exclude an item from the Spotlight search

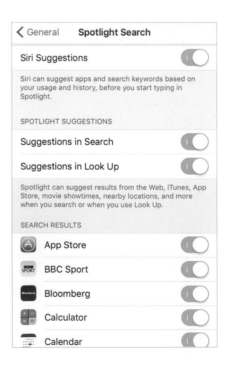

Accessing Spotlight

The Spotlight Search box can be accessed from any Home screen by pressing and swiping downwards on any free area of the Home screen. This also activates the keyboard.

Enter the name of an app into the Spotlight Search box and tap on the result to launch the app from here.

1 Enter a keyword or phrase into the Search box. The results appear under the Search box as you type and become more defined as you add information

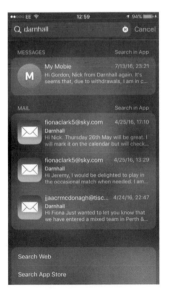

2 In iOS 10, Spotlight can not only search over your iPhone but also over the App Store and the web. It can return results for restaurants nearby, or movie times if you enter the name of a movie (this varies depending on geographical locations)

Beware

There is no separate headphone jack on the iPhone 7. Instead, headphones are connected via the Lightning Connector jack. However, this means that earphones and headphones with a traditional jack will not work with the iPhone 7, unless the Lightning to 3.5mm headphone jack adapter is used (this is included with the iPhone 7 and 7 Plus).

Both models of the iPhone 7 can be used with the AirPods the wireless headphones from Apple.

Using the EarPods

The iPhone EarPods are not only an excellent way to listen to music and other audio on your iPhone, they can also be used in a variety of ways with the phone function:

The EarPods contain three main controls:

Down volume   Up volume

Central control button

- Plug in the EarPods to use them to hear someone who is calling you. Speak normally and the other person will be able to hear you via the EarPods' in-built microphone.

- Click once in the middle of the control button to answer an incoming call.

- Press and hold in the middle of the control button for a couple of seconds (until you hear two beeps) to decline an incoming call.

- Click once in the middle of the control button to end the current call.

- If you are on a call and receive another one, click once on the middle of the control button to put the first call on hold and activate the second call.

- Press and hold the middle of the control button to dial a number using Voice Control, whereby you can speak the required number.

- Click on the control button when playing a music track to pause it. Click again to restart it. Double-click on the control button to move to the next track. Triple-click on the control button to move back to the previous track.

3 Head in the iCloud

iCloud, the online storage service, is at the heart of the iPhone for backing up your content and sharing it with other family members.

What is iCloud?

iCloud is the Apple online storage and backup service that performs a number of valuable functions:

- It makes your content available across multiple devices. The content is stored in the iCloud and then pushed out to other iCloud-enabled devices, including the iPad, iPod Touch and other Mac or Windows computers.

- It enables online access to your content via the iCloud website. This includes your iCloud email, photos, contacts, calendar, reminders and documents.

- It can back up the content on your iPhone.

To use iCloud you must have an Apple ID and register for iCloud. Both of these things can be done when you first set up your iPhone, or at a later date.

Once you have registered for and set up iCloud, it works automatically so you do not have to worry about anything.

1 Tap once on the **Settings** app

2 Tap once on the **iCloud** tab

3 Enter your Apple ID and password to set up iCloud on your iPhone

4 If you do not yet have an Apple ID, tap once on the **Create a new Apple ID** button and follow the steps to create your Apple ID

‹ Settings	iCloud
	nickvandome@mac.com
	••••••••
Sign In	
Create a new Apple ID	
An Apple ID is the login you use for just about everything you do with Apple.	

iCloud Settings

Once you have set up your iCloud account you can then apply settings for how it works. Once you have done this you will not have to worry about it again:

1 Tap once on the **iCloud** tab in Settings

2 Drag these buttons to **On** for each item that you wish to be included in iCloud. Each item is then saved and stored in the iCloud and made available to your other iCloud-enabled devices

Once you have set up an iCloud account, your iCloud email address appears on the iCloud button in Step 1.

Adding iCloud Storage

By default, you get 5GB of free storage space with an iCloud account. However, you can upgrade this if you want to increase the amount of storage. To do this:

Hot tip

If you have a lot of photos stored in iCloud then you may want to consider increasing your amount of storage.

1 Access **iCloud** in Settings

2 Tap once on the **Storage** button to view how your iCloud storage is being used

Hot tip

Another useful iCloud function is the iCloud Keychain (**Settings** > **iCloud** > **Keychain**). If this is enabled, it can keep all of your passwords and credit card information up-to-date across multiple devices and remember them when you use them on websites. The information is encrypted and controlled through your Apple ID.

3 Tap once on the **Buy More Storage** button if you want to increase the amount of iCloud storage

4 Tap once on one of the storage options to buy this amount of iCloud storage (Note: charges appear in your local currency)

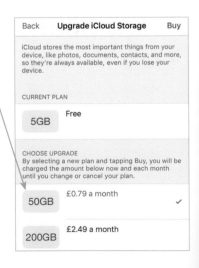

Backing up with iCloud

All of the items that you have assigned to iCloud (see page 55) should be backed up there automatically. However, if this is not happening you may need to turn on the iCloud Backup. To do this:

1 Within the iCloud section of the Settings app, tap once on the **Backup** button, if it is Off

2 The iCloud Backup button will be **Off**

3 Drag the **iCloud Backup** button to **On** to enable automatic backup for iCloud. This has to be done over Wi-Fi with the iPhone locked and plugged in

4 You can also back up manually at any time by tapping once on the **Back Up Now** button

Hot tip

You can also back up your iPhone to a computer that has iTunes. Connect the iPhone to the computer with the Lightning/USB cable and open iTunes. Click on this button on the top toolbar and, under the **Summary** tab, click on the **Back Up Now** button under the **Manually Back up and Restore** heading.

About Family Sharing

As everyone gets more and more digital devices it is becoming increasingly important to be able to share content with other people, particularly family members. In iOS 10, the Family Sharing function enables you to share items that you have downloaded from the App Store, such as music and movies, with up to six other family members, as long as they have an Apple Account. Once this has been set up, it is also possible to share items such as family calendars, photos and even see where family members are with Find My Friends. To set up and start using Family Sharing, access the iCloud section within the Settings app, as shown on page 54.

Beware

To use Family Sharing, the other members of the group need to have iOS 8 (or later) installed on their mobile devices, or OS X Yosemite (or later) on an Apple desktop or laptop computer.

58

1   Tap once on the **Set Up Family Sharing...** link

2   Tap once on the **Get Started** button

3   One person will be the organizer of Family Sharing, i.e. in charge of it, and if you set it up then it will be you. Tap once on the **Continue** button (the Family Sharing account will then be linked to your Apple ID)

4 Tap once on the **Continue** button again

5 If you are the organizer of Family Sharing, payments for items will be taken from the credit/debit card that you registered when you set up your Apple ID. Tap once on the **Continue** button

6 Once Family Sharing has been created, return to the iCloud section in the Settings app and tap once on the **Add Family Member...** button

7 Enter the name or email address of a family member and tap once on the **Next** button

8 An invitation is sent to the selected person. They have to accept this before they can participate in Family Sharing

Hot tip

When you invite someone to Family Sharing you can specify that they have to ask permission before downloading content from the iTunes Store, the App Store or the iBooks Store. To do this, select the family member in the **Family** section of the **iCloud** settings and drag the **Ask To Buy** button to **On**. Each time they want to buy something you will be sent a notification asking for approval. This is a good option if grandchildren are added to the Family Sharing group.

Using Family Sharing

Once you have set up Family Sharing and added family members you can start sharing a selection of items.

Sharing photos

Photos can be shared with Family Sharing thanks to the Family album that is created automatically within the Photos app. To use this:

Beware

iCloud Photo Sharing has to be turned **On** to enable Family Sharing for photos (**Settings** > **Photos & Camera** > **iCloud Photo Sharing**).

60

Hot tip

When someone else in your Family Sharing circle adds a photo to the Family album, you are notified in the Notification Center and also by a red notification on the Photos app.

1 Tap once on the **Photos** app

2 Tap once on the **Shared** button

3 The **Family** album is already available in the **Shared** section. Tap once on the blank album and start adding photos to it

Family
From You

4 Tap once on this button to add photos to the album

5 Tap once on the photos you want to add and tap once on the **Done** button

6 Make sure the **Family** album is selected as the Shared Album and tap once on the **Post** button

Sharing calendars

Family Sharing also generates a Family calendar that can be used by all Family Sharing members:

1 Tap once on the **Calendar** app

2 Tap once on this button to create a New Event. The current calendar will probably not be the Family one. Tap once on the calendar to change it

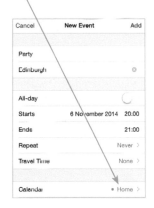

3 Tap once on the **Family** calendar

4 The **Family** calendar is now selected for the event

Calendar	● Family >

5 Complete the details for the event. It will be added to your calendar, with the **Family** tag. Other people in your Family Sharing circle will have this event added to their Family calendar too, and they will be sent a notification

Don't forget

When someone in the Family Sharing circle adds an event to the Family calendar it will appear in your calendar with the appropriate tag. A red notification will also appear on the Calendar app and it will appear in the Notification Center (if the Calendar has been selected to appear here).

Don't forget

Tap once on the **Add** button to invite other people by email (they do not have to be part of Family Sharing, but they do have to accept your invitation to be part of Find My Friends).

Add

Don't forget

Tap once on your own name at the bottom-left of the screen to see your settings for Find My Friends. This is where you can share your location. Share My Location also has to be turned on within **Settings** > **Privacy** > **Location Services** > **Share My Location**.

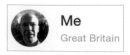

Me
Great Britain

...cont'd

Finding family members

Family Sharing makes it easy to keep in touch with the rest of the family and see exactly where they are. This can be done with the Find Friends app. The other person must have their iPhone (or other Apple device) turned on, be online and be sharing their location. To do this:

1 Tap once on the **Find Friends** app

2 Your own location has to be shared if you want other people to see it. Tap once on the **Me** button at the bottom of the window and drag the **Share My Location** button to On

3 The details of any people who are linked via your Family Sharing are displayed. Tap once on a person's name to view their details and location in the top panel (if they are online and have shared their location on their device)

Sharing apps, music, books and movies

Family Sharing means that all members of the group can share purchases from the iTunes Store, the App Store or the iBooks store. To do this:

1 Open either **iTunes Store**, **App Store** or **iBooks**

2 Tap once on the **Purchased** button

3 Your own purchases are listed under **My Purchases**

4 Tap once on someone under **Family Purchases** to view their purchases

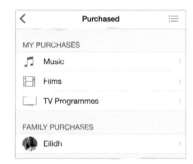

5 The person's purchases are listed. Tap on the buttons at the top of the window to view different categories

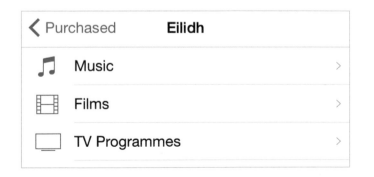

6 Tap once on this button next to an item to download it to your iPhone

Using Family Sharing, other members of the group will be able to access and download the content that you have purchased too.

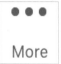

Depending on the app, there may be an additional step before the **Purchased** button can be accessed. In the iTunes Store, this is the **More** (**...**) button;

More

in the App Store, it is the **Updates** button.

Don't forget

Pages is used for word processing, Numbers for spreadsheets and Keynote for presentations. They can all be downloaded, for free, from the App Store.

Don't forget

Once iCloud Drive is set up for specific apps, you will be able to create a document on your iPhone and then continue working on it on another compatible device, such as a MacBook or an iPad. The iCloud Drive app can be used to access the documents that are stored in the iCloud Drive.

iCloud Drive

Linking It All Up

Once iCloud is set up, all of the items that you have turned On in Settings will automatically be stored and backed up to the iCloud. If you open them on another iCloud-enabled device, you will be able to work with the latest version that has been created.

So, if you have started a note in the Notes app on your iPhone you will be able to open it on an iPad (with your own iCloud account) and continue where you left off. This is known as continuity.

Using iCloud Drive

It is also possible to have the same continuity for other apps, such as the Apple suite of productivity apps: Pages, Numbers and Keynote. This is done with the iCloud Drive feature.

1 Access **iCloud** in the Settings app

☁ iCloud
nickvandome@mac.com

2 Tap once the **iCloud Drive** button

☁ iCloud Drive   Off ›

3 Drag the **iCloud Drive** button to **On**

4 Drag **On** the buttons for any compatible apps that you want to use with iCloud Drive

4 Calls and Contacts

One of the main uses for the iPhone is still to make and receive phone calls. This chapter shows what you need for this.

Adding Contacts

Because of its power and versatility it is sometimes forgotten that one of the reasons for the iPhone's existence is to make phone calls. Before you start doing this, it is a good idea to add family and friends to the Contacts app. This will enable you to phone them without having to tap in their phone number each time. To add a contact:

1 Tap once on the **Contacts** app

2 Any contacts that you already have are displayed

3 Tap once on this button to add a new contact

Don't forget

Tap once on the green button next to a field to add another field. Tap once on a red button to delete a field.

4 Enter the name for the contact at the top of the window, in the **First name** and **Last name** fields

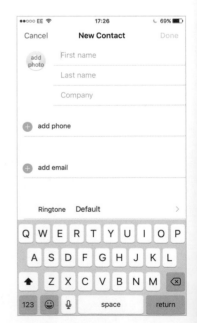

5 Tap once in one of the Phone fields, or tap once on the **add phone** button to add a new Phone field

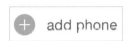

6 Enter the required number with the number pad that is activated when you tap in a Phone field

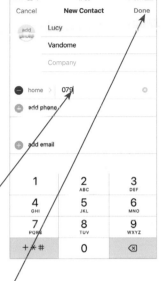

7 Tap once on the **Done** button to add the new contact

8 The contact is added under **Contacts**

9 Tap once on a contact to view their full details. You can use these buttons at the top of the window to send them a text, make a voice call to them, make a video, or voice, call using FaceTime or send them an email (if their email address is included)

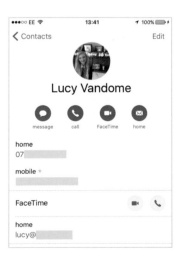

Hot tip

Use the buttons at the bottom of a contact's window to send them a message, share their details with other people, add them as a favorite or share your location with them. If someone is added as a favorite, they can be accessed directly from the **Favorites** button on the bottom toolbar of the **Phone** app.

Making a Call

The iPhone 7 can be used to make calls to specific phone numbers that you enter manually, or to contacts in your Contacts app.

Dialing a number

To make a call by dialing a specific number, first tap once on the **Phone** app.

You must have a SIM card inserted in your iPhone and an appropriate cellular/mobile service provider in order to make a call with the **Phone** app.

1 Tap once on the **Keypad** button at the bottom of the window

Tap once on the Voicemail button on the bottom toolbar to view any messages here. If you have any, there will be a red notification icon on the Voicemail button.

2 Tap on the numbers on the keypad to enter the number, which appears at the top of the window. Tap on this button to delete a number that has been entered

3 Tap once on this button to make the call

Calling a contact

To call someone who has been added to the Contacts app:

1 Open the **Phone** app and tap once on the **Contacts** button at the bottom of the window. The Contacts app opens, with the Phone toolbar still visible at the bottom of the window

Contacts

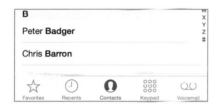

2 Tap once on a contact

3 The full details for the contact are displayed. Tap once on the **call** button at the top of the window to call the number of the contact

call

Hot tip

To find someone in the Contacts app (either directly from the app, or from the **Contacts** button in the Phone app), swipe up and down on the screen; enter a name in the Search box at the top of the window; or tap on a letter on the alphabetic list down the right-hand side.

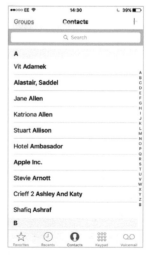

Receiving a Call

When you receive a call, there are four main options:

Don't forget

When a call is connected, the following buttons appear on the screen. Use them to: mute a call; access the keyboard again, in case you need to add any more information, such as for an automated call; access the speaker so you do not have to keep the phone at your ear; add another call to create a conference call; make a FaceTime call to the caller (if they have this facility); or access your Contacts app.

1 When you receive a call, the person's name and photo (if they have been added to your Contacts), or number, appears at the top of the screen

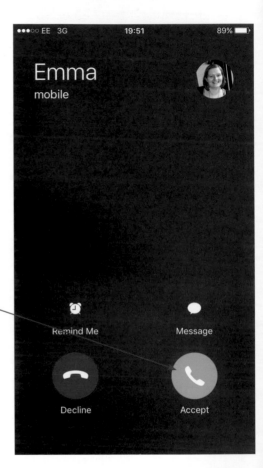

2 Tap once on the **Accept** button (or if the phone is locked, drag the **slide to answer** button to the right) to take the call

3 Tap once on the **Decline** button to decline the call, without any other actions. If the phone is locked when a call comes in, press the phone's **On/Off** button to decline the call. This is then displayed at the top of the window:

4 Tap once on the **Remind Me** button to decline the call but set a reminder for yourself that the person has called

5 Select an option for when you want to be reminded

The reminder in Step 5 will appear on the Lock screen and also as a notification in the Notification Center (if this has been specified).

6 Tap once on the **Message** button to decline the call but send the person a text message instead (see page 76 for details on setting this up)

7 Tap once on the text message that you want to send

Tap once on this button to end a call.

Saving Phone Contacts

Another quick way to add a contact is to ask someone to phone you so that you can then copy their number directly from your phone to your Contacts. You do not even have to answer the phone to do this.

1 Once someone has phoned, tap once on the **Phone** app

2 Tap once on the **Recents** button at the bottom of the window

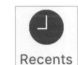

3 The call will be displayed. Tap once on the **i** symbol

4 Information about the call is displayed, including the number

Information from a caller can also be added to an existing contact. For instance, if one of your contacts calls you from a different phone, these details can be added to their existing information. To do this, tap once on the **Add to Existing Contact** button in Step 5.

5 Tap once on the **Create New Contact** button

6 The New Contact window opens, with the number already pre-inserted

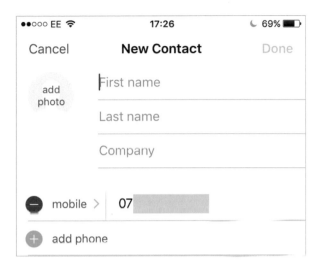

7 Add information for the contact, as required, such as name, any additional phone numbers and email

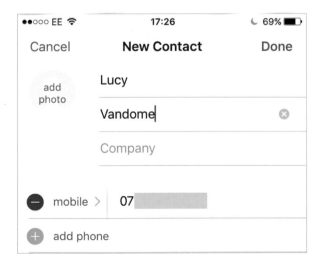

8 Tap once on the **Done** button to add the new contact

Done

Setting Ringtones

Ringtones were one of the original 'killer apps' for mobile/cell phones: the must-have accessory that helped transform the way people looked at these devices. The iPhone has a range of ringtones that can be used and you can also download and install thousands more. To use the default ringtones:

1 Tap once on the **Settings** app

2 Tap once on the **Sounds** tab

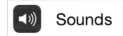

3 Tap once on the **Ringtone**

link under Sounds and Vibration Patterns to select ringtones for when you receive a phone call

4 Tap once on one of the options to hear a preview and select it

5 Ringtones can also be selected for a range of other items, such as email, FaceTime calls, Facebook posts and calendar and reminder alerts, by going back to the Sounds and Vibration Patterns section and choosing a tone for each item

Hot tip

Tap once on the **Store** button in the top right-hand corner of the Ringtone window to go to the iTunes Store where you can download more ringtones, from the **Tones** button.

74

Adding individual ringtones

It is also possible to set ringtones for individual people, so that you know immediately who a call is from.

1 Select a contact in the Contacts app and tap on the **Edit** button

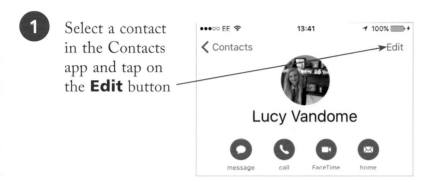

2 Tap once on the **Ringtone** button

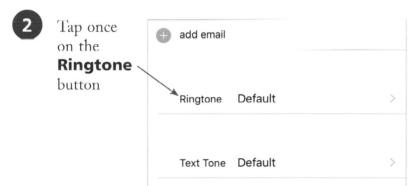

3 Tap once on a ringtone to assign this to the contact

Only set ringtones for your most regular contacts, otherwise you may end up with too many variations.

Phone Settings

As with most of the iPhone functions, there is a range of settings for the phone itself. To use them:

1 Tap once on the **Settings** app

2 Tap once on the **Phone** tab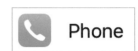

3 The Phone settings have options for responding with a text to a call that you do not take, call forwarding, call waiting and blocking unwanted callers

4 Tap once on the **Respond with Text** button to create a text message that can be sent if you do not want to answer a call when it is made

5 Typing and Texts

This chapter shows how to get used to the virtual keyboard for adding text, and how to use the texting options, including the range of items that can be added for text messages with iOS 10.

The iPhone Keyboard

The keyboard on the iPhone is a virtual one, i.e. it appears on the touchscreen whenever text or numbered input is required for an app. This can be for a variety of reasons:

- Entering text with a word processing app, or into an email or an organizing app such as Notes.

- Entering a web address in a web browser such as the Safari app.

- Entering information into an online form.

- Entering a password.

Viewing the keyboard

When you attempt one of the actions above, the keyboard appears so that you can enter any text or numbers:

Shift button

Space bar

Around the keyboard

To access the various keyboard controls:

1 Tap once on the **Shift** button to create a **Cap** (capital) text letter

2 Double-tap on the **Shift** button to create **Caps Lock**

3 Tap once on this button to back delete an item

Hot tip

In some apps, such as Notes, Mail and Messages, it is possible to change the keyboard into a trackpad for moving the cursor. To do this, press and hold firmly on the keyboard and then swipe over the trackpad to move the cursor around.

Hot tip

It is possible to increase the size of the iPhone keyboard with the **Zoom** feature within the Accessibility settings. See pages 180-181 for details.

Don't forget

To return from Caps Lock, tap once on the **Caps** button.

78

4 Tap once on this button to access the **Numbers** keyboard option

5 From the Numbers keyboard, tap once on this button to access the **Symbols** keyboard

6 Tap once on this button on either of the two keyboards above to return to the standard QWERTY option

Shortcut keys

Instead of having to go to a different keyboard every time you want to add punctuation (or numbers) there is a shortcut for this:

1 Press and hold on the **Numbers** button and swipe over the item you want to include. This will be added and you will remain on the QWERTY keyboard

> **Hot tip**
>
> If you are entering a password, or details into a form, the keyboard will have a **Go** or **Send** button that can be used to activate the information that has been entered.

> **Hot tip**
>
> Several keys have additional options that can be accessed by pressing and holding on the key. A lot of these are letters that have accented versions in different languages, e.g. a, e, i, o and u. Swipe across a letter to add it.

Keyboard Settings

Settings for the keyboard can be determined in the General section of the Settings app. To do this:

Drag the **Predictive** button to **On** to enable predictive texting (see pages 82-83).
Drag the **Character Preview** button to **On** to show a magnified example of a letter or symbol when it is pressed, to ensure that the correct one is selected.

1. Tap once on the **Settings** app

2. Tap once on the **General** tab

3. Tap once on the **Keyboard** link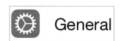

4. Drag the **Auto-Capitalization** button to **On** to automatically capitalize letters at the beginning of a sentence

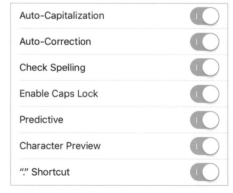

Auto-Capitalization	
Auto-Correction	
Check Spelling	
Enable Caps Lock	
Predictive	
Character Preview	
"." Shortcut	

The Auto-Correction function works as you type a word, so it may change a number of times, depending on the length of the word you are typing.

5. Drag the **Auto-Correction** button to **On** to enable suggestions for words to appear as you type, particularly if you have mistyped a word

6. Drag the **Check Spelling** button to **On** to identify misspelled words (with red underlining)

7. Drag the **Enable Caps Lock** button to **On** to enable this function to be performed

8. Drag the **"." Shortcut** button to **On** to add a period (full stop) and a space to start a new sentence by just tapping the space bar twice

9 Tap once on **Text Replacement** link to view existing text shortcuts and also to create new ones

With iOS 10, third-party keyboards can be downloaded from the App Store and used instead of the default one. Two to look at are SwiftKey Keyboard and Swype.

10 Tap once on this button to create new shortcuts

11 Enter a phrase and the shortcut you want to create it when you type. Tap once on the **Save** button

By default, two keyboards are installed: one for the language of your region and the emoji one. If more keyboards are added, this symbol will appear on the keyboard. Press on it to select another keyboard from the one being used. If only the two default keyboards are installed, this symbol will be the emoji one.

12 Tap once on the **Keyboards** button in Step 9 to add a new keyboard

13 Tap once on the **Add New Keyboard...** button

Add New Keyboard...

14 Tap once on a keyboard to add it. The keyboard will be available by selecting the globe icon (see tip)

Using Predictive Text

Predictive text tries to guess what you are typing and also predicts the next word following the one you have just typed. It is excellent for text messaging.

To use it:

1 Tap once on the **General** tab in the Settings app

2 Tap once on the **Keyboard** link

Keyboard	>

3 Drag the **Predictive** button **On**

Predictive	⬤

4 When predictive text is activated, the QuickType bar is displayed above the keyboard. Initially, this has a suggestion for the first word to include. Tap on a word or start typing

5 As you type, suggestions appear. Tap on one to accept it. Tap on the word within the quotation marks to accept exactly what you have typed

Don't forget

Predictive text learns from your writing style as you write and so gets more accurate at predicting words. It can also recognize a change in style for different apps, such as Mail and Messages.

6 If you continue typing, the predictive suggestions will change as you add more letters

7 After you have typed a word, a suggestion for the next word appears. Tap on one of the suggestions, or start typing a new word, which will then also have predictive suggestions as you type

Toggling predictive text from the keyboard
You can also toggle predictive text On or Off from the keyboard. To do this:

1 Press and hold on this button on the keyboard

2 Drag the **Predictive** button to turn it **On** or **Off**

Hot tip

Tapping the button in Step 1 allows you to add Emojis, which are symbols used in text messages to signify happiness, surprise, sadness, etc. (See page 92 for details.)

Entering Text

Once you have applied the keyboard settings that you require you can start entering text. To do this:

If you keep typing as normal, the Auto-Correction suggestion will disappear when you finish the word.

1 Tap once on the screen to activate the keyboard from the app. Start typing with the keyboard. The text will appear at the point where you tapped on the screen

2 As you type, Auto-Correction comes up with suggestions (if it is turned on). Tap once on the space bar to accept the suggestion, or tap once on the cross next to it to reject it

If Predictive text is turned **On** (**Settings > General > Keyboard > Predictive**) the auto-correction suggestions will appear on the QuickType bar above the keyboard.

3 If Check Spelling is enabled in the keyboard settings, any misspelled words appear underlined in red

The **"."Shortcut** option has to be turned **On** (**Settings > General > Keyboard > "." Shortcut**) for the functionality in Step 4 to work (see page 80).

4 Double-tap the space bar to enter a period (full-stop) and a space at the end of a sentence

Editing Text

Once text has been entered it can be selected, copied, cut and pasted. Depending on the app being used, the text can also be formatted, such as with a word processing app.

Selecting text

To select text and perform tasks on it:

1 To change the insertion point, tap and hold until the magnifying glass appears

2 Drag the magnifying glass to move the insertion point

3 Tap once at the insertion point to access the selection buttons

Hot tip

Once the selection buttons have been accessed, tap once on **Select** to select the previous word, or **Select All** to select all of the text.

...cont'd

4 Double-tap on a word to select it. Tap once on **Cut** or **Copy** as required

Hot tip

The selection buttons in Steps 4 and 5 can also be used to replace the selected word, add bold, italics or underlining to it, view a definition (Look Up) of it, share it or indent it. (These options may change depending on the app you're in, and whether the iPhone is held in portrait or landscape mode.)

5 Tap once here to view additional options

6 Drag the selection handles to expand or contract the selection

Voice Typing

On the keyboard there is also a voice typing option, which enables you to enter text by speaking into a microphone, rather than typing on the keyboard. This is On by default.

Using voice typing

Voice typing (dictation) can be used with any app with a text input function. To do this:

1 Tap once on this button on the keyboard to activate the voice typing microphone. Speak into the microphone to record text

2 As the voice typing function is processing the recording, this screen appears

3 Tap once on the **Done** button to finish recording

4 Once the recording has been processed, the text appears in the app

Beware

Voice typing is not an exact science and you may find that some strange examples appear. The best results are created if you speak as clearly as possible and reasonably slowly.

Hot tip

Dictation can be turned **On** or **Off** in **Settings** > **General** > **Keyboard** > **Enable Dictation**.

Don't forget

There are other voice typing apps available from the App Store. One to try is Dragon Dictation.

Types of Text Messages

Text messaging should not be thought of as the domain of the younger generation. On your iPhone you can join the world of text with the Apple iMessage service that is accessed via the Messages app. This enables text, photo, video and audio messages to be sent, free of charge, between users of iOS (version 5 onwards) on the iPhone, iPad, iPod Touch, and Mac computers with OS X or macOS.

However, there are two different types of text messages:

- iMessages that are sent over Wi-Fi, to other users with an Apple ID and using an iPhone, iPad, iPod Touch or a Mac computer.

- Text messages that are just sent via your cellular (mobile) carrier.

Wi-Fi texts (iMessages)

When texts are sent over Wi-Fi this can only be done with other users who have an Apple ID.

When you are connected to Wi-Fi this symbol appears at the top of your iPhone.

To use iMessages over Wi-Fi, the **iMessage** button has to be **On**, in the **Messages** section of the Settings app.

Cellular (mobile) carrier texts (SMS)

When texts are sent via your mobile carrier, this can be done to any cellular (mobile) number.

When you are connected to your cellular (mobile) carrier this symbol appears at the top of your iPhone, with the appropriate carrier's name.

In the Messages settings there is also an option to send texts as SMS when iMessages is unavailable. However, since this will then be sent using your cellular network, a charge may apply for the text.

88

Sending an iMessage via Wi-Fi

When you send an iMessage it appears in a blue bubble.

Sending a text via your carrier

When you send a text via your cellular (mobile) carrier, it appears in a green bubble.

If you enter a number that is not connected to an Apple ID account then the message will be sent as an SMS (green bubble) rather than an iMessage (blue bubble).

Text Messaging

The process for sending text messages is the same for either iMessages or SMS text messages:

1 Tap once on the **Messages** app

2 You have to sign in with your Apple ID before you can use Messages. Enter these details and tap on the **Sign In** button

3 Tap once on this button to create a new message and start a new conversation

4 Tap once on this button to select someone from your contacts

5 Tap once on a contact to select them as the recipient of the new message

Don't forget

You can also enter a cell/mobile phone number into the To field for text messages in Messages. If this is connected to an Apple ID, the message will be sent as an iMessage; if not, it will be sent as an SMS message.

Hot tip

You can also add someone from your contacts by typing their name into the **To:** field shown in Step 4. As you start typing, names will appear for you to select from. You can type the telephone number of anyone who isn't in your contacts here, too.

6 Tap once here and type with the keyboard to create a message

When a message has been sent, you are notified underneath it when it has been delivered.

7 Tap once on this button to send a message (it is not available until a message has been composed)

Press and hold on a message and tap on the **More...** button that appears. Select a message, or messages, and tap on the **Trash** icon to remove them from the threads. (See pages 99-100 for more information on deleting messages.)

8 As the conversation progresses, each message is displayed in the main window

Enhancing Text Messages

Adding emojis

Emojis (small graphical symbols) are becoming more common in text messages and there is now a huge range that can be included with iOS 10. To do this:

The effects on the next seven pages require the recipient to be using iMessages and iOS 10 too. Otherwise, the messages may appear differently, or not have the same animated effects.

Don't forget

Emojis are grouped together, according to subject. These include Smileys & People, Animals & Nature, Food & Drink, Objects and Flags.

Hot tip

Turn Predictive text On in the Keyboard settings (see page 82) to get emoji suggestions as you type.

1 Tap once on this button on the keyboard to view the emoji keyboards

2 Swipe left and right to view the emoji options. Tap once on an emoji to add it to a message

Emojis can be added automatically from certain words:

1 Add text and tap once on the button in Step 1 above. The items that can be replaced are highlighted

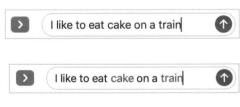

2 Tap once on a highlighted word to see the emoji options. Tap once on one to add it to the message

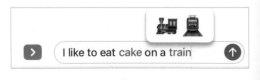

Full-screen messages

iMessages can also be sent with full-screen effects:

1 Write a message and press and hold on this button

2 Tap once on the **Screen** button at the top of the window

Screen

Hot tip

Some messages, such as 'Happy Birthday' and 'Congratulations' automatically create full-screen effects.

3 Different animated options can be selected to accompany the message

4 Swipe to the left, or tap on these buttons to view different animated effects

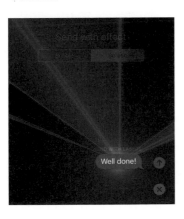

5 Tap once on this button to send the message (tap once on the cross to delete the animated effect)

While creating a message, tap once here for the options for adding additional types of content, including adding stickers, digital touch items and photos (see pages 96-98).

The other Bubble effects in Step 2 are Slam, Loud and Gentle. These determine how the speech bubble appears to the recipient: Slam moves in quickly from left to right; Loud appears initially as a large bubble; Gentle appears initially with small text in the speech bubble. After the initial effects, the bubble returns to its normal size.

...cont'd

Invisible messages

There are several ways to enhance text messages, including sending them in a digital version of invisible ink:

1 Write a message and press on this button

2 Tap once on the **Bubble** button at the top of the window

Bubble

3 Tap once on the **Invisible Ink** button

4 Tap once on this button to send the invisible message

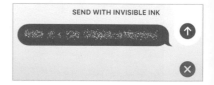

5 The message is sent as a bubble where the content is obscured

6 Swipe on the message to view its content

This is a top secret message!

Handwritten messages

To create a more informal message, handwriting can be used.

1 Turn the iPhone into landscape mode and tap once on this button on the keyboard to access the handwriting panel

2 Write using your finger or select one of the pre-formatted messages at the bottom of the panel. Tap once on the **Done** button to add it to a message. The text appears animated to the recipient, as if it is being written on their screen

Quick replies (Tapback)

Instead of writing a full reply to a message it is possible to add a quick reply (also known as Tapback), which consists of an appropriate icon that is attached to the original message:

1 Press and hold on the message to which you want to add a quick reply and tap once on one of the icons

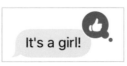

2 The selected icon is added to the original message and this is displayed to the sender of the message

If the button in Step 1 is not showing, tap once on this button to the left of the text field box.

Music and photos can also be added from the button in Step 4, using the Images and Music buttons (the images are the pre-loaded ones, rather than those from your own photo library; see next page).

...cont'd

Adding stickers

Stickers and graphics are another option for enhancing text messages. To do this:

1 Tap once on this button to the left of the text field box

2 Swipe left and right to see the content that is already available, including a range of images

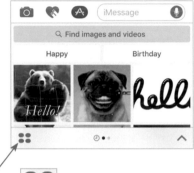

3 Tap once on this button

4 Tap once on the **Store** button to view sticker sets in the App Store

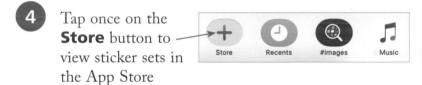

5 Navigate the stickers section in the App Store to find a set of stickers as required. Swipe up the screen to see the full range of sticker categories

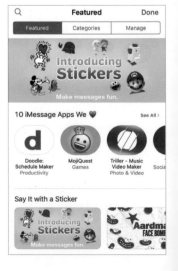

6 Tap once the **Get** button next to a sticker set to download it

If a sticker set is a paid-for option, the button in Step 6 will have a price on it.

7 The sticker set will be added to the panel in Step 2 on the previous page. Tap on a sticker to add it to a message. Tap once on the cross next to a sticker to delete it, after it has been added to a message

You can also send family and friends audio clips in an iMessage so that they can hear from you too. To do this, press and hold on the microphone icon at the right-hand side of the text field and record your message.

Adding photos and videos

To add photos or videos to a message:

1 Tap once on this button to the left of the message text field to add a photo or video, either by taking it from the iPhone's **Camera** app or by selecting one from your **Photo Library**

...cont'd

Digital Touch

Graphical effects can also be added to messages, with the Digital Touch option:

1 Tap once on this button

2 Select one of the Digital Touch options from the right-hand side of the panel to add a graphical effect. These include sketching with one finger (tap once on the colored circle at the left to select a color), tapping with one finger to create a circle, pressing with one finger to create a fireball, tapping with two fingers to create a kiss, and tapping and holding with two fingers to create a heartbeat. The effect is sent in a message

3 Tap once on this button to draw over a photo

4 Select a color at the top of the window and draw over the image on the screen. Tap once on these buttons to capture, from left to right, a photo or a video (this can be done before or after the drawing has been applied)

Draw before or during recording

Hot tip

With Messages you can show people your location (by sending a map) rather than just telling them. To do this: Once a conversation has started, tap once on the **i** button at the top of the message window. Tap once on the **Send My Current Location**, or **Share My Location** buttons.

Send My Current Location

Share My Location

For **Share My Location**, options can be selected for **Share for One Hour**, **Share Until End of Day** or **Share Indefinitely**. If you select **Share My Location**, this will be updated if your location changes (as long as Location Services is turned On in **Settings** > **Privacy** > **Location Services**).

Managing Messages

Text conversations with individuals can become quite lengthy so it is sometimes a good idea to remove some messages, while still keeping the conversation going.

1 As a conversation with one person progresses, it moves downwards in the window

Hot tip

You can copy a message by tapping once on the **Copy** button in Step 2 and then pasting it into another app, such as an email. To do this, press and hold on an open email and tap once on the **Paste** button.

2 Press and hold on a message that you want to delete and tap once on the **More...** button (pressing and holding on a message also activates the Tapback option; see page 95)

3 Tap once next to any message that you want to delete, so that a white tick in a blue circle appears

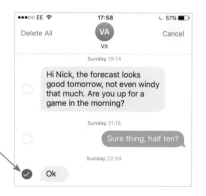

Hot tip

Settings for the Messages app can be applied in the Settings app. These include: Send Read Receipts, to indicate that you have read the message sent, and to send SMS messages when iMessage is unavailable.

4 Tap once on the Trash icon to delete the selected message(s)

...cont'd

Whole conversations can also be deleted:

1 From a conversation, tap once on the **Back** button to view all of your conversations

2 Tap once on the **Edit** button

It is good housekeeping to delete conversations that have finished, otherwise you may end up with a long list of different ones.

3 Tap once next to any whole conversation(s) that you want to delete

Cancel		Messages	
✓	RF	**Richard Frenz** — Yesterday	
		Badders on Thursday at 6pm 2 courts booked. Can you manage?	
✓	MC	**Martin Campbell** — Yesterday	
		Good stuff, the forecast is not bad for then, but we'll see what transpi...	
○		**Lucy** — Thursday	
		Cool, see you then xxx	
✓	VA	**Vit Adamek** — Wednesday	
		Yup looks okay!	

4 Tap once on the **Delete** button at the bottom right-hand corner of the screen to remove the selected conversation(s)

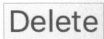

6 The Online World

This chapter shows how to use your iPhone to keep ahead in the fast-moving world of online communications, using the web, email, social media and video calls.

Getting Online

Connecting to Wi-Fi is one of the main ways that the iPhone can get online access. You will need to have an Internet Service Provider and a Wi-Fi router to connect to the internet. Once this is in place, you will be able to connect to a Wi-Fi network:

You can also get online access through your cellular network, which is provided by your phone network supplier. However, data charges may apply for this.

1 Tap once on the **Settings** app

Settings

2 Tap once on the **Wi-Fi** tab

🛜 Wi-Fi   Not Connected ›

3 Ensure the **Wi-Fi** button is in the **On** position

4 Available networks are shown here. Tap once on one to select it

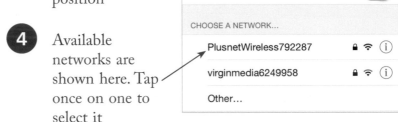

‹ Settings   Wi-Fi

Wi-Fi

CHOOSE A NETWORK...

PlusnetWireless792287   🔒 🛜 ⓘ

virginmedia6249958   🔒 🛜 ⓘ

Other...

If you are connecting to your home Wi-Fi network, the iPhone should connect automatically each time, after it has been set up. If you are connecting in a public Wi-Fi area you will be asked which network you would like to join.

5 Enter a password for your Wi-Fi router

Enter the password for "PlusnetWireless792287"

Cancel   **Enter Password**   Join

Password   ●●●●●●●●●●

6 Tap once on the **Join** button   Join

7 Once a network has been joined, a tick appears next to it. This now provides access to the internet

‹ Settings   Wi-Fi

Wi-Fi

✓ PlusnetWireless792287   🔒 🛜 ⓘ

Safari Settings

Safari is the default web browser on the iPhone 7 and it can be used to bring the web to your iPhone. Before you start using Safari, there is a range of settings that can be applied:

1 Tap once on the **Settings** app

2 Tap once on the **Safari** tab

3 Make selections under the **Search** section for the default search engine, options for suggestions appearing as you type search words and phrases, and preloading the top-rating page in a search

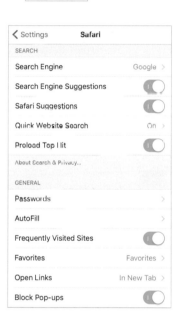

4 Make selections under the **General** section for entering passwords, specifying the items for the Favorites window, and blocking pop-ups

5 Make selections under the **Privacy & Security** section for blocking cookies, warning about fraudulent websites, checking to see whether websites accept Apple Pay and clearing your web browsing history and web data

Because of the proliferation of apps available for the iPhone, you may find that you use Safari less than on a desktop or laptop computer. For example, most major news outlets have their own apps that can be used as standalone items, rather than having to use Safari to access the site. Look for apps for your favorite websites in the App Store, as a shortcut for accessing them quickly.

Web Browsing with Safari

To start browsing the web with Safari and enjoy the variety of the information within it:

Don't forget

The **Share** button in Step 5 can be used to share a web page via Message, Mail or social media sites such as Facebook or Twitter. It can also be added to a Note.

Hot tip

If you have a Twitter account added to your iPhone (see page 114), it can be linked to Safari so that you can view your Twitter feed here. To do this, tap once on the **Bookmarks** button in Step 6. Tap once on the button below and tap once on the **Subscriptions** button. Drag the Twitter account button to **On**.

1 Tap once on the **Safari** app

2 Enter a website address here in the Address Bar, or tap once on one of the items in the Favorites window

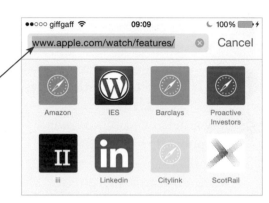

3 As you type in the Address Bar, website suggestions appear and also search suggestions with Google

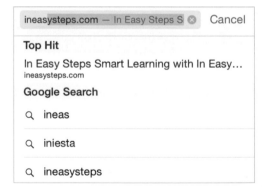

4 When you access a web page, use these buttons to visit the Next and Previous pages

5 Use this button to share a web page

6 Use this button to view bookmarks

7 Use this button to view, add and delete tabs (see pages 106-107)

Adding bookmarks

Everyone has favorite websites that they visit, and in Safari it is possible to mark these with bookmarks so that they can be accessed quickly. To do this:

1 Tap once on this button on the bottom toolbar

2 Tap once on the **Add Bookmark** button

3 Select a name and location for the bookmark and tap once on the **Save** button

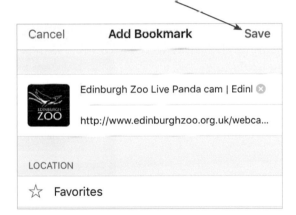

4 Tap once on the **Bookmarks** button and tap once here to view your bookmarks

If the bottom toolbar is not visible on a web page, swipe downwards on the page to view it.

The **Bookmarks** button in Step 4 can also be used to access any reading list items that have been stored. These are added from the **Share** button in Step 1 and enables items to be saved and read later, even if you are not connected to the internet.

Using Tabs in Safari

In keeping with most modern web browsers, Safari uses tabs so that you can have several websites open at the same time. However, due the fact that a smartphone's screen is smaller than those on a desktop or laptop computer, tabs operate in a specific way on the iPhone. To use tabs:

Hot tip

Press and hold on a tab to drag it into a different position in Tab View.

Press and hold the Tab button to get the option to close all open tabs in one go.

Don't forget

Tap once on the **Done** button at the bottom of the Tab View window to exit this and return to the web page that was being viewed when Tab View was activated.

1 Open Safari and open a website

2 Tap once on this button on the bottom toolbar to view all currently open tabs

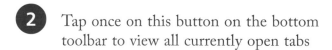

3 Swipe up and down in Tab View to view all of the open tabs. Tap once on one to view that web page at full size

4 Swipe to the bottom of the page to view any tabs that you have open on any other Apple devices, such as an iPad

Opening tabs

To open more tabs in Safari on your iPhone:

1 Open the Tab View window as shown on the previous page and tap once on this button

2 Open the new tab by entering a web address in the Address Bar, or by tapping once on one of the items in the Favorites window

3 Tap once on the **Private** button in Tab View to open a new tab that is not recorded in your web history

Private

4 Open the private tab in the same way as a regular one. This is indicated by a dark bar at the top of the window

5 Tap once on this button to close any tab in Tab View

Setting up an Email Account

Email accounts

Email settings can be specified within the Settings app. Different email accounts can also be added there.

1 Tap once on the **Settings** app

2 Tap once on the **Mail** link

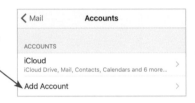

3 Tap once on the **Accounts** link

4 Tap once on the **Add Account** button to add a new account

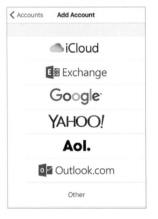

5 Tap once on the type of email account you want to add

If your email provider is not on the **Add Account** list, tap once on **Other** at the bottom of the list and complete the account details using the information from your email provider.

6 Enter the details for the account and tap on the **Next** button to move through the wizard

...cont'd

7 Drag these buttons **On** or **Off** to specify which functions are to be available for the required account. Tap once on the **Save** button

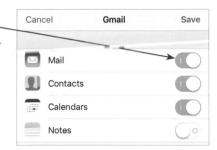

8 Each new account is added under the **Accounts** heading of the Mail section

If you set up more than one email account, messages from all of them can be downloaded and displayed by **Mail**.

Email settings

Email settings can be specified within the Settings app:

1

1 Under the Mail section there are several options for how Mail operates and looks. These include how much of an email will be previewed in your Inbox and options for accessing actions by swiping on an email

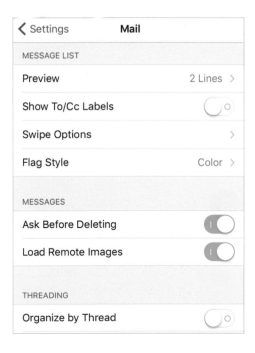

The **Organize by Thread** option can be turned **On** to show connected email conversations within your Inbox. If there is a thread of emails this is indicated by this symbol.

Tap on it once to view the thread.

Emailing

Email on the iPhone is created, sent and received using the Mail app (although other mail apps can be downloaded from the App Store). This provides a range of functionality for managing emails and responding to them.

Accessing Mail

To access Mail and start sending and receiving emails:

Use these buttons at the top of the window when you are reading an email to view the Next and Previous messages.

1 Tap once on the **Mail** app (the red icon in the corner displays the number of unread emails in your Inbox)

2 Tap once on a message to display it in the main panel

If the **Fetch New Data** option in the **Mail** > **Accounts** settings is set to **Push**, new emails will be downloaded automatically from your mail server. To check manually, swipe down from the top of the mailbox pane. The Push option uses up more battery power.

3 Use these buttons to, from left to right, flag a message, move a message to a specific folder, delete a message, respond to a message and create a new message

4 Tap once on this button to reply to a message, reply to everyone in a conversation, forward it to a new recipient, or print it

Reply

Reply All

Forward

Print

Cancel

To delete an email from your Inbox, swipe on it from right to left and tap once on the **Trash/Delete** button.

Press and hold in the body text area to get the option to attach photos/videos to your email. Photos can also be attached to an email by opening them in the **Photos** app, tapping once on the **Share** button and selecting the **Mail** option.

Creating email

To create and send an email:

1 Tap once on this button to create a new message

2 Enter a recipient name in the **To** box

Cancel	Lunch	Send
To: Eilidh Vandome		
Cc/Bcc, From: nickvandome@me.com		
Subject: Lunch		
Hi, where would you like to go?		
Sent from my iPhone		

3 Enter a subject and body text

4 Tap once on the **Send** button to send the email to the recipient

If the recipient is included in your Contacts app, their details will appear as you type in Step 2. Tap once on the email address, if it appears, to include it in the **To** field of a new email.

111

Having a Video Chat

Video chatting is a very personal and interactive way to keep in touch with family and friends around the world. The FaceTime app provides this facility with other iPhone, iPad and iPod Touch users, or a Mac computer with FaceTime. To use FaceTime for video chatting:

1 Tap once on the **FaceTime** app

2 Recent video chats are shown under the **Video** tab. Tap once here to select a contact

3 Tap once on a contact to access their details for making a FaceTime call

4 Tap once on their phone number or email address to make a FaceTime call. The recipient must have FaceTime on their iPhone, iPad, iPod Touch or Mac computer, or

5 Tap once on these buttons next to a contact to make a video or audio call

6 Once you have selected a contact, FaceTime starts connecting to them and displays this at the top of the screen

7 When you have connected, your contact appears in the main window and you appear in a picture-in-picture thumbnail in the corner

Hot tip

The contacts for FaceTime calls are taken from the iPhone Contacts app. You can also add new contacts directly to the contacts list by tapping once on the + sign and adding the relevant details for the new contact.

113

8 Tap once on this button to swap between cameras on your iPhone

9 Tap once on this button to end the FaceTime call

10 If someone else makes a call to you, tap once on the **Decline** or **Accept** buttons

Adding Social Media

Using social media sites such as Facebook, Twitter and Flickr to keep in touch with families and friends has now become common across all generations. On the iPhone with iOS 10 it is possible to link to these accounts so that you can share content to them from your iPhone, and also view updates through the Notification Center. To set up social media accounts on your iPhone:

Hot tip

Updates can be set to appear in your **Notification Center**. Open **Settings** and tap once on the **Notifications** tab. Under the **Notification Style** heading, tap once on the social media site and select options for how you would like the notifications to appear.

Don't forget

Social media sites can be accessed from their own apps on the iPhone and also from their respective websites using Safari.

1 Tap once on the **Settings** app

2 Select the required social media option in the left-hand panel

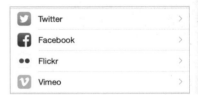

3 Tap on the **Install** button to download the relevant app

INSTALL

4 Enter your login details for your account, or tap on the **Create New Account** button

5 Once you have set up your account, tap once on the **Share** button, where it is available, such as in the Photos app, to share content with your social media sites

7 Hands on with Apps

Apps are the items that give the iPhone instructions on the tasks to be performed. This chapter details the pre-installed apps and also shows how to access those in the App Store.

Don't forget

You need an active internet connection to download apps from the App Store.

Hot tip

Within a number of apps there is a **Share** button that can be used to share items through a variety of methods, including iMessages, email, Facebook and Twitter.

What is an App?

An app is just a more modern name for a computer program. Initially, it was used in relation to mobile devices such as the iPhone and the iPad, but it is now becoming more widely used with desktop and laptop computers, for both Mac and Windows operating systems.

On the iPhone there are two types of apps:

● **Pre-installed apps**. These are the apps that come already installed on the iPhone.

● **App Store apps**. These are apps that can be downloaded from the online App Store. There is a huge range of apps available there, covering a variety of different categories. Some are free, while others have to be paid for. The apps in the App Store are updated and added to on a daily basis so there are always new ones to explore.

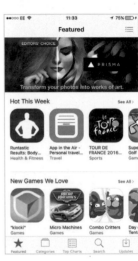

There are also two important points about apps (both pre-installed and those from the App Store) to remember:

● Apart from some of the pre-installed apps, the majority of apps do not interact with each other. This means that there is less chance of viruses being transmitted from app to app on your iPhone, and they can operate without a reliance on other apps.

● Content created by apps is saved within the app itself, rather than within a file structure on your iPhone, e.g. if you create a note in the Notes app, it is saved there; if you take a photo, it is saved in the Photos app. Content is usually also saved automatically when it is created, or edited, so you do not have to worry about saving it as you work on it.

Pre-installed Apps

The pre-installed iPhone apps are the ones that appear on the Home screen when you first get your iPhone:

- **App Store**. This can be used to access the online App Store, from where additional apps can be downloaded and updated.

- **Calculator**. This is a basic calculator, which can also be accessed from the Control Center.

- **Calendar**. An app for storing appointments, important dates and other calendar information. It can be synced with iCloud.

- **Camera**. This gives direct access to the front-facing and rear-facing iPhone cameras.

- **Clock**. This displays the current time and can be used to view the time in different countries. It also has an alarm clock and a stopwatch.

- **Compass**. This can be used to show you the direction of North. You can give the compass access to your location so that you can follow it from where you are.

- **Contacts**. An address book app. Once contacts are added here they can then also be accessed from other apps, such as Mail.

- **FaceTime**. This app uses the front-facing FaceTime camera to hold video or audio chats with compatible Apple devices.

- **Find My Friends**. This can be used to view the location of family and friends, based on their Apple mobile devices and Mac computers.

Hot tip

Some of the default apps are located on the second Home screen, within the **Extras** folder.

Don't forget

Some of the pre-installed apps, such as Mail and Contacts, interact with each other. However, since these are designed by Apple there is a limited chance of them containing viruses.

117

Hot tip

If you don't want your contacts to be accessed by other apps then open **Settings** > **Privacy** > **Contacts** and drag the button for these apps to Off.

...cont'd

You need an Apple ID to obtain content from the iTunes Store and iBooks.

- **Find My iPhone**. This can be used to locate your iPhone and other Apple devices. It is set up in **Settings** > **iCloud**.

- **Health**. This stores and collates a range of health information. See pages 134-135.

- **Home**. This is a new app in iOS 10 that can be used to control certain compatible functions within the home, such as heating controls.

- **iBooks**. This is an app for downloading electronic books, which can then be read on the iPhone.

- **iCloud Drive**. This is used to back up items and make them available to other Apple devices.

- **iTunes Store**. This app can be used to browse the iTunes Store, where content can be downloaded to your iPhone.

- **Mail**. This is the email app for sending and receiving email on your iPhone.

- **Maps**. Use this app to view maps from around the world, find specific locations and get directions to destinations.

- **Messages**. This is the iPhone messaging service, which can be used for SMS text messages and iMessages between compatible Apple devices.

- **Music**. An app for playing music on your iPhone and also viewing cover artwork. You can also use it to create your own playlists.

- **News**. This collates news stories from numerous online publications and categories.

- **Notes**. If you need to jot down your thoughts or ideas, this app is perfect for just that.

- **Photos**. This is an app for viewing and editing your photos and videos, and creating slideshows. It can also be used to share photos via iCloud, email, iMessage and social media.

- **Podcasts**. This can be used to download podcasts from within the App Store and then play them on your iPhone.

- **Reminders**. Use this app to help keep organized, when you want to create to-do lists and set reminders for events.

- **Safari**. The Apple web browser that has been developed for viewing the web on your iPhone.

- **Settings**. This contains a range of settings for the iPhone (see pages 18-19 for details).

- **Stocks**. Information about stocks and shares. You can add your own favorites.

- **Tips**. This can be used to display tips and hints for items on your iPhone.

- **Videos**. This is an app for viewing videos that you have purchased from the iTunes Store, and also streaming them to a larger HDTV monitor.

- **Voice Memos**. This can be used to record short audio reminders that can be stored and played on the iPhone.

- **Wallet**. This can be used to store credit, debit and store-card details, for making payments with Apple Pay (in some locations).

- **Watch**. This can be used to pair an iPhone with the Apple Watch and apply a range of settings for it.

- **Weather**. Displays weather details for your location and destinations around the world.

Don't forget

A podcast is an audio or video program and they cover an extensive range of subjects.

About the App Store

While the pre-installed apps that come with the iPhone are flexible and versatile, apps really come into their own when you connect to the App Store. This is an online resource and there are thousands of apps there that can be downloaded and then used on your iPhone, including categories from Lifestyle to Medical and Travel.

To use the App Store, you must first have an Apple ID. This can be obtained when you first connect to the App Store. Once you have an Apple ID you can start exploring the App Store and the apps within it:

1 Tap once on the **App Store** app on the Home screen

2 The latest available apps are displayed on the Homepage of the App Store, including the featured and best new apps

3 Tap on these buttons to view the apps according to **Featured**, **Categories**, **Top Charts**, and **Updates**

Don't forget

The items within the Featured section of the App Store change on a regular basis, so it is always worth looking at it from time to time.

Viewing apps

To view apps in the App Store and read about their content and functionality:

1 Tap once on an app

2 General details about the app are displayed

3 Swipe left or right here to view additional information about the app and view details

If it is an upgraded version of an app, this page will include details of any fixes and improvements that have been made.

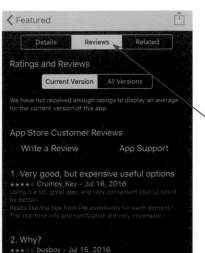

4 Reviews and related apps are available from the relevant buttons, next to the **Details** button

Finding Apps

Featured

Within the App Store, apps are separated into categories according to type. This enables you to find apps according to particular subjects. To do this:

1 Tap once on the **Featured** button on the toolbar at the bottom of the App Store

2 Scroll left and right to view items within each section heading

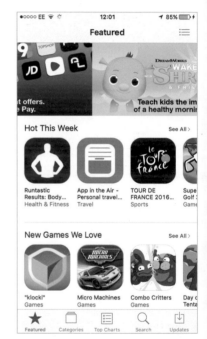

3 Scroll up the page to view additional sections and **Quick Links**

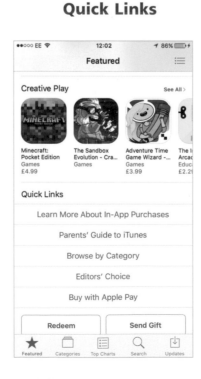

4 Tap once on the **Categories** button on the toolbar at the bottom of the window to view the specific categories

5 Tap once on a category to view the items within it. This can be navigated in the same way as the main Featured page in the App Store, e.g. swipe up and down to view sections and left and right on each panel to view the available apps

Hot tip

Tap once on the **See All** link next to a section within a category to view all of the apps in that section.

...cont'd

Top Charts
To find the top-rated apps:

1 Tap once on the **Top Charts** button on the toolbar at the bottom of the App Store window

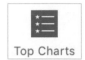

2 The top overall paid-for, free and top-grossing apps are displayed

Do not limit yourself to just viewing the top apps. Although these are the most popular, there are also a lot of excellent apps within each category.

3 To find the top apps in different categories, tap once on the **Categories** button

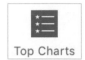

Categories

4 Tap once on a category

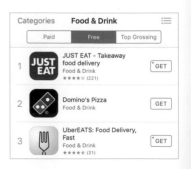

5 The top apps for that category are displayed

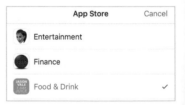

Searching for apps

Another way to find apps is with the App Store Search box, which appears at the top of the App Store window once it has been accessed. To use this to find apps:

1 Tap on the **Search** button at the bottom of the window to access the Search box

2 Tap in the Search box to activate the keyboard and enter a search keyword or phrase

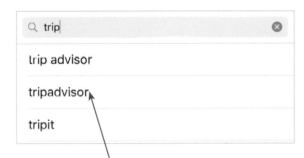

3 Suggested apps appear as you are typing

4 Tap on an app to view it

For more information about using the iPhone virtual keyboard, see Chapter Five.

Downloading Apps

When you identify an app that you would like to use, it can be downloaded to your iPhone. To do this:

Apps usually download in a few minutes, or less, depending on the speed of your Wi-Fi connection.

Some apps have 'in-app purchases'. This is additional content that has to be paid for when it is downloaded.

1 Find the app you want, using the **App Store**

2 Tap once on the **Price** or **Get** button

3 Tap once on the **Install** button

4 Enter the password for your Apple Id and tap once on the **OK** button. The app will install

Sign In to iTunes Store

Touch ID requires your password when iPhone restarts. Enter the password for "nickvandome@mac.com".

Password

Cancel   OK

Updating Apps

The publishers of apps provide updates, which bring new features and improvements. You do not have to check your apps to see if there are updates – you can set them to be updated automatically through the Settings app. To do this:

1 Open **Settings** and tap on the **iTunes & App Store** tab

You should keep your apps as up-to-date as possible to take advantage of software fixes and any updates to the iPhone operating system (iOS).

2 Drag the **Updates** button under **Automatic Downloads** to **On** to enable automatic updates for apps

Managing your Apps

As more apps are added it can become hard to find the ones you want, particularly if you have to swipe between several screens. However, it is possible to organize apps into individual folders to make using them more manageable. To do this:

1 Press on an app until it starts to jiggle and a cross appears at the top-left corner. (The cross can be used to delete the app – see next page)

2 Drag the app over another one

3 A folder is created, containing the two apps. The folder is given a default name, usually based on the category of the first app

4 Tap once on the folder name and type a new name if required

5 Tap on the **Done** button on the keyboard or click on the **Home** button to finish creating the folder

6 Click the **Home** button again to return to the Home screen (this is done whenever you want to return to the Home screen from an app's folder)

7 The folder is added on the Home screen. Tap on this to access the items within it

Deleting Apps

If you decide that you do not want certain apps anymore, they can be deleted from your iPhone. However, they remain in the iCloud so that you can reinstall them if you change your mind. This also means that if you delete an app by mistake, you can get it back from the App Store without having to pay for it again. To do this:

1 Press on an app until it starts to jiggle and a cross appears at the top-left corner

2 Tap once on the cross to delete the app. In the Delete dialog box, tap once on the **Delete** button

Delete "Bloomberg"?
Deleting this app will also delete its data.

Cancel	Delete

3 To reinstall a deleted app, tap once on the **App Store** app

4 Tap once on the **Updates** button

Beware

If you delete an app it will also delete any data that has been compiled with that app, even if you reinstall it from the App Store.

NEW

Hot tip

Most of the pre-installed apps can now be deleted, using iOS 10. The ones that cannot be deleted are: App Store, Camera, Clock, Find My iPhone, Health, Messages, Phone, Photos, Safari, Settings and Wallet.

...cont'd

5 Tap once on the **Purchased** button

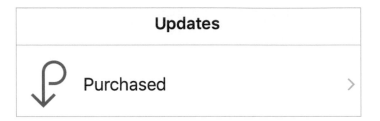

6 Tap once on the **My Purchases** button to view all of your purchased apps

All of the apps that you have downloaded, including those on other Apple devices, will be listed in the My Purchases section of the App Store.

7 Tap once on the **iCloud** button to reinstall an app

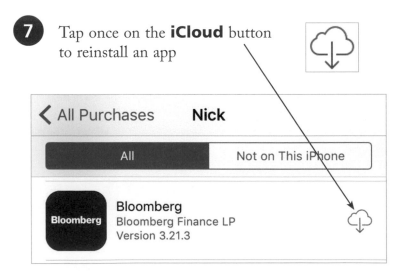

8 Apps for Every Day

The iPhone 7 has apps to make your day-to-day life run more efficiently and smoothly.

Health Options on the iPhone

The Health app

Health and general fitness is of interest to many of us and the iPhone 7 recognizes this with a range

of apps designed to help us stay in good health and monitor our health activities. One way in which this is done is with the Health app. This can be used to store a range of health information, from how much sleep you get each night, to your cholesterol level. Data can be entered for regular time periods, and charts are produced for days, weeks, months and years. This enables you to build up an accurate picture of your health needs and activities. Other health apps can also communicate with the Health app so that more information can be aggregated.

Working with the Apple Watch

In April 2015, Apple introduced the Apple Watch, and the Apple Watch 2 was released in September 2016. This is much more than a watch, though: it is also a body monitoring device. It has a number of sensors on the back which monitor information such as heart rate and body movement. There is also an activity app to measure your fitness activities. A lot of this data can be sent to the Health app on the iPhone, where it can be stored and analyzed in greater depth. Wearable technology like the Apple Watch is undoubtedly a growth area and there are likely to be more and more health and fitness features added as this technology evolves.

Wearable devices are beginning to capture the public's imagination and this will undoubtedly develop more in the future, particularly as they are used more in conjunction with body sensors and health and fitness apps.

The Apple Watch has to be used in conjunction with an iPhone 6 (or later) to activate its full range of functionality. It is 'paired' with an iPhone using the Watch app.

App Store health and fitness apps

The App Store not only has a wide range of health and fitness apps, it even has a whole category for them:

1 Tap once on the **App Store** app

2 Tap once on the **Categories** button

3 Tap once on the **Health & Fitness** category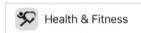

4 The **Categories** button displays the currently-recommended apps: tap once on the **Top Charts** button to view the top free and paid-for health and fitness apps

Some health and fitness apps are free, but they then offer in-app purchases for additional features.

The App Store also has a **Medical** category.

If you have a pre-existing medical condition, or are on any medication, always consult your doctor before using a new health or fitness app that could have an impact on this.

Using the Health App

The Health app is available in iOS 10 and it enables you to input and analyze a wide range of health and fitness information. There are four main areas:

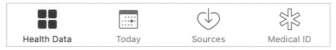

Health Data   Today   Sources   Medical ID

New apps designed to interact with the Health app are being produced by a number of different developers and the range will grow over time.

- **Health Data**. This displays the available categories within the Health App.

- **Today**. This displays health data that has been collated for specific days.

Tap on the calendar at the top of the Today window to view data from different dates. The current date is indicated by a red circle.

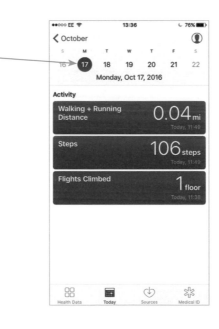

Some items in the Health App have data added automatically, such as Walking + Running, Steps, and Flights Climbed, in the Activity category. Other items need to have their data added manually (see next page).

- **Sources**. This displays information from any other health apps on your iPhone, providing they have requested access to the Health app.

- **Medical ID**. This can be used to add your own medical information such as medical conditions, allergies, blood type and emergency contacts.

Adding health data

To enter a range of information into the Health App:

1 Tap once on the **Health Data** button

2 Tap once on one of the main categories

3 Tap once on one of the sub-categories, e.g. Caffeine in the Nutrition category

4 Tap once on this button to add data for the selected item

5 Add the data for the selected item and tap once on the **Add** button

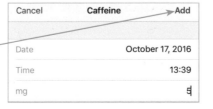

Here, you get the option to enter your personal data and medical details. It'll be well worth entering these for emergencies.

When adding data, do so at regular intervals, otherwise the results and analysis may not be complete.

Once data has been added it is shown on the graph in Step 4. Add data for more categories, as required.

Jotting Down Notes

It is always useful to have a quick way of making notes of everyday things, such as shopping lists, recipes or packing lists for traveling. On your iPhone, the Notes app is perfect for this function. To use it:

1 Tap once on the **Notes** app

2 Tap once on this button on the bottom toolbar to create a new note

3 Enter text for the note

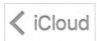

4 Tap once on this button to share (via Message or Mail, or any social media apps on your iPhone), copy or print a note

5 Tap once on this button to access the formatting toolbar. (Tap once on the cross to close the toolbar)

6 Double-tap on text to select it and tap once on this button to access text formatting options

Formatting	Done
Title	
Heading	
Body	

Don't forget

For more information about selecting text, see pages 85-86.

7 Tap once on this button to create a checklist. Add items to the list. Tap once on a check button to add a tick and show it as completed ⊘

Hot tip

Press and hold firmly on the keyboard in Notes to activate it as a trackpad. You can then swipe over it to move the cursor around the screen. This can also be done in the Mail and Messages apps.

137

8 Tap once on this button to share the current note and allow someone else to edit it

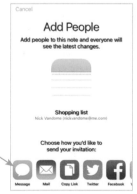

9 Select how you want to share the note, e.g. Message, Mail or a social media app

NEW

10 Enter any additional text as required and send the message. The recipient will then be able to access the note and edit it (if they have a compatible device)

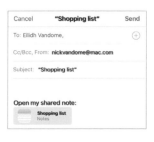

...cont'd

11 Tap once on this button to add a handwritten item or drawing

12 Select a drawing object at the bottom of the screen and draw on the screen. Tap once on the **Done** button. The drawing is added to the current note

Don't forget

Tap once on this icon on the bottom toolbar to delete the current note.

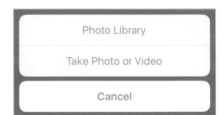

13 Tap once on this button to add a photo or video to a note. Select a photo or video from your library, or take a new one

| Photo Library |
| Take Photo or Video |
| Cancel |

14 The latest note appears at the top of the iCloud list. Each time a note is edited, it moves to the top

| ‹ | **iCloud** | Edit |

My latest note
14:31 Update ideas

iPad for Seniors iOS 10
14:31 No additional text

Keeping Up-to-Date

The Calendar can be used to add events and appointments and keep yourself up-to-date with your daily, monthly and annual activities.

1 Tap once on the **Calendar** app

2 If **Month** view is displayed, tap once here to access **Year** view. In Year view, tap once on a month to view it

3 Tap once on a day to view it (the current day is highlighted red)

Tap once on the **Today** button from any date to view the current date, in whichever view you are currently in.

4 Swipe up and down to view any events in **Day** view. Tap once on an event to view its details

...cont'd

Adding events

To add new events to the calendar:

Hot tip

Drag the **All-day** button to **On** to set an event for the whole day, rather than adding specific start and end times.

Don't forget

The repeat frequency for an event can be set to every day, every week, every 2 weeks, every month or every year. There is also a **Custom** option for specific time periods.

1 Press and hold on a timeslot within Day view, or tap once on this button

2 Enter a title for the event and tap once on the **Starts** button to add a start time

3 Add an end time, by tapping on the **Ends** button, and also a repeat frequency (for recurring events such as birthdays). Select a specific calendar for the event and add an alert, if required. Tap once on the **Add** button to create the event

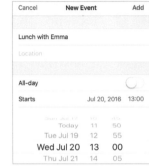

4 Tap once on this button to view a list of your current events and appointments

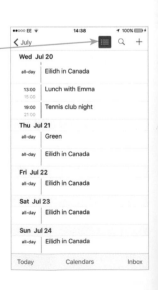

Getting the News

The iPhone with iOS 10 is ideal for keeping up with the news, whether you are on the move or at home. This is made even easier with the News app, which can be used to collate news stories from numerous online media outlets, covering hundreds of subjects. To use it:

1 Tap once on the **News** app

2 Tap once on the **Explore** button to select topics to populate the news feed

3 Tap once on the cross on an item to add it

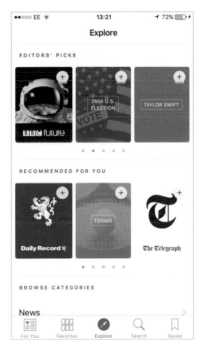

4 Tap once on the **Favorites** button on the bottom toolbar to view the publications that were added in Step 3

Hot tip

To delete an item from the Favorites section, tap once on the **Edit** button in the top right-hand corner and tap on the cross next to the item you want to delete. This will remove its related content from your news feed.

...cont'd

5 Tap once on the **For You** button to view the news feed from selected publications and subjects. Tap here to view the full selection for the main heading (e.g. Top Stories)

6 Scroll down the main For You page to view top-trending topics within the News app

Hot tip

Tap once on the **Search** button on the bottom toolbar to look for specific publications or subjects. These can then be added to your news feed and will appear under the **For You** and **Favorites** sections.

Search

7 When an article has been opened for reading, tap once these buttons on the bottom toolbar to, from left to right: share it; remove it from favorites; add it to favorites; or save it

8 Saved items can be accessed from this button on the News app's Home screen

Saved

9 Relaxing with your iPhone

This chapter shows how to get the most out of your iPhone for playing music and reading, and also how to shop and research online.

Around the iTunes Store

The iPhone performs an excellent role as a mobile entertainment center: its versatility means that you can carry your music, videos and books in your pocket. Most of this content comes from the online iTunes Store. To access this and start adding content to your iPhone:

Tap once on the **Genres** button at the top of the Music Homepage to view items for different musical genres and styles.

Tap once on the **Charts** tab to view the top-ranking items for the category that is being viewed.

1 Tap once on the **iTunes Store** app

2 The iTunes Store interface is similar to the App Store. Tap once on the **Featured** or **Charts** tabs at the top of the window to view these headings

3 Use the buttons on the bottom toolbar to access content for Music, Films/Movies and TV Programmes/Shows

4 Swipe to the left and right on each panel to view items within it

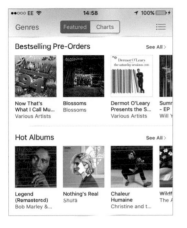

5 Swipe up and down to view more headings

Downloaded movies and TV shows take up a lot of storage space on the iPhone.

6 Tap once on the **Films/Movies** button to view the movies in the iTunes Store. These can be bought or rented

7 Tap once on the **TV Programmes/Shows** button to view the TV shows in the iTunes Store. These can be bought or rented

8 Tap once on a **More** button to access additional content

9 Tap once on the **Genius** button to view suggested content, based on what you have already bought from the iTunes Store

To view all of your iTunes purchases, tap once on the **More** button on the bottom toolbar and tap once on the **Purchased** button. View your purchases by category (Music, Films/Movies or TV Programmes/ Shows) and tap once on the cloud symbol next to a purchased item to download it to your iPhone.

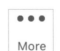

Buying Items

Once you have found the content you want in the iTunes Store, you can then buy it and download it to your iPhone.

If you have set up Apple Pay (see pages 42-45) you will be able to use this to buy items in the iTunes Store. Use the Touch ID function (see page 25) in Step 1, after you have tapped on the price button, to authorize the payment using Apple Pay.

1 For music items, tap once on the price button next to an item (either an album or individual songs) and follow the instructions. Tap once on the **Music** app to play the item (see next page)

2 For movies and TV shows, tap once on the **Buy** or **Rent** button next to the title. Tap once on the **Videos** app to play the item

For rented movies and TV shows you have 30 days to watch an item after you have downloaded it. After you have started watching, you have 48 hours until it expires.

Playing Music

Once music has been bought from the iTunes Store it can be played on your iPhone using the Music app. To do this:

1 Tap once on the **Music** app

2 Tap once on the **Library** button on the bottom toolbar

3 Select one of the options for viewing items in the Library. This can be **Playlists**, **Artists**, **Albums**, **Songs** and **Downloaded Music**

To create a playlist of songs, tap once on the **Playlists** button in Step 3, then tap once on the **New Playlist...** button. Give it a name and then add songs from your Library, using the **Add Music** button.

147

4 For the **Artists** section, tap once on an artist to view details of their songs on your iPhone

...cont'd

Don't forget

Tap once on this button in Step 5 to access a menu for the current track. This includes options to download the track, delete it from the Music app Library, add it to a playlist, or add it to the queue of music to be played.

Don't forget

By default, music that has been bought from the iTunes Store is kept online and can be played on your iPhone by streaming it over Wi-Fi. However, it is also possible to download tracks to your iPhone so that you can play them without being online. Tap once on this button to download a specific track.

5 Select a track to play it

6 A limited version of the music controls appears at the bottom of the window

7 Tap once here to view the full version of the music controls. Use these buttons to return to the start of a track, play/ pause a track, fast forward and adjust the volume

Using Apple Music

Apple Music is a service that makes the entire Apple iTunes library of music available to users. It is a subscription service, but there is a three month free trial. Music can be streamed over the internet or downloaded so you can listen to it when you are offline. To start with Apple Music:

1 Tap once on the **Music** app

2 Tap once on the **For You** button

3 Tap once on the **Choose Your Plan** button. (This option is available if you have already used the free, three-month trial of Apple Music)

4 Select the type of plan to which you want to subscribe and tap once on the **Join Apple Music** button. Once you have joined Apple Music you will be able to select the music genres in which you are most interested and receive suggestions based on this. You will also be able to listen to the entire iTunes Library of music

To end your Apple Music subscription at any point (and to ensure you do not subscribe at the end of the free trial) open the **Settings** app. Tap once on the **iTunes & App Store** button and tap once on your own **Apple ID** link (in blue). Tap once on the **View Apple ID** button and enter your Apple ID password. Under **Subscriptions** tap once on the **Manage** button. Drag the **Automatic Renewal** button to **Off**. You can then renew your Apple Music membership, if required, by selecting one of the **Renewal Options**. If you do not renew your subscription once the free trial finishes, you will not be able to access any music that you have downloaded during the trial.

149

Reading

In addition to audio and visual content from the iTunes Store, it is also possible to read books on your iPhone, using the iBooks app. To do this:

1 Tap once on the **iBooks** app

2 Tap once on the **My Books** button on the bottom toolbar to view any items you have in your Library

Hot tip

Although not as large as a book, or an electronic book reader, both the iPhone 7 and iPhone 7 Plus are acceptable for reading books. The larger iPhone 7 Plus is the better option, but the high-quality Retina screen on both models means that it is an option for reading, particularly if you are traveling.

3 If a title has a cloud icon next to it, tap once on this to download the book to your iPhone

4 Tap once on the **Featured** button on the bottom toolbar to view books in the iBooks Store

5 The **Featured** interface of the iBooks Store is similar to that for the iTunes Store. Swipe up and down, or left and right, to view the content in the iBooks Store. Tap once on the **Top Charts** button on the bottom toolbar to view the top-selling titles in different categories

Top Charts

Hot tip

If you have a Kindle account, you can download the Kindle app from the App Store and use this to connect to your account and all of the books within it.

Kindle
AMZN Mobile LLC
★★★★★ (15)

6 Once books have been downloaded to your iPhone, tap once on a title in the **My Books** section to read it. Tap on the left or right of the screen to move between pages, or swipe from the left or right edges. Tap in the middle of a page to activate the reading controls at the top of the screen, including table of contents, text size, and color options

151

Shopping

Online shopping was one of the first great commercial successes on the web. Thousands of retailers now have their own websites and, increasingly, their own apps that can be used on the iPhone. So there are now more options than ever for online shopping:

Don't forget

For some online retailers, you will have to register and create an account before you can buy items. For others, you will be able to go straight to the checkout and enter your payment details.

Don't forget

A number of online retailers offer Apple Pay (see pages 42-45) as a method of payment, denoted by the Apple Pay logo. The number of retailers offering this is likely to grow considerably, as Apple Pay becomes more widely available.

1 Download apps from the App Store for well-known retailers such as Amazon and eBay

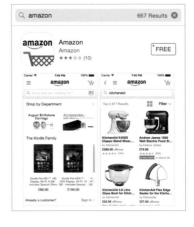

2 Use Safari and look up the retailer's website (in some cases the website will have an option to download the app too)

3 For some websites they will only enable you to download the retailer's app and use this

Comparing prices

Online retailing has also made it a lot easier to compare prices between sites. This can be done in two main ways:

1 Use Safari and search for price comparison websites. Different sites specialize in different products and services, so you may want to use a number of them

Another option for comparing prices is to check them in a bricks-and-mortar shop and then compare them with the online prices.

2 There are apps in the App Store that can be used to scan barcodes of products and then compare prices for a specific item across different retailers

Researching

With your iPhone in your hand you literally have a world of information at your fingertips. Whatever your hobby or interest, you will be able to find out a lot more about it using several different options:

1 Press and hold on the **Home** button to access **Siri** and make an enquiry this way

2 Use the **App Store** to search for apps for your chosen subject

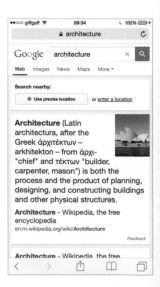

3 Search **Safari** to find related websites and also general information about a specific topic

Don't forget

By default, the search engine used by Safari is Google. However, this can be changed in **Settings** > **Safari** > **Search Engine**.

154

10 On the Go

The iPhone 7 is a great companion whenever you are out and about anywhere, whether at home or abroad.

Finding Locations

Finding locations around the world is only ever a couple of taps away when you have your iPhone and the Maps app.

1 Tap once on the **Maps** app

2 The Search box is at the bottom of the window

3 Enter an item into the Search box. As you type, suggestions appear underneath. Tap on one to go to that location

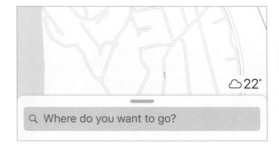

4 For the currently-selected location, options for searching over items such as food outlets, shops and

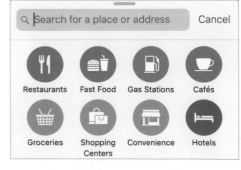

entertainment are available. Tap on one of these to see results for these in the current location

5 The location selected in Step 3 is displayed, with information about it at the bottom of the window

Some locations have a 3D Flyover Tour feature. This is an automated tour of a location, featuring its most notable sites. It covers major cities around the world and the list is regularly being added to. If it is available for a location, tap once on the **Flyover Tour** button at the bottom of the window, next to the **Directions** button. Try it with a location such as New York, London or Paris.

157

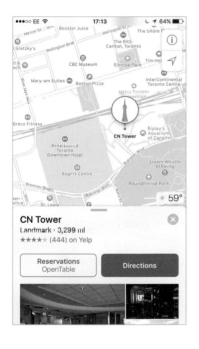

6 Swipe up from the bottom of the window to view full details about the location, including photos, address, phone number and website address, if available

7 At the top of the Maps app window, tap once on this icon for map style options

8 Select either **Standard (Map)**, **Transit** or **Satellite** to view the map in that style

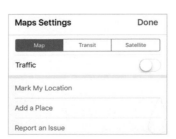

Getting Directions

Wherever you are in the world, you can get directions between two locations. To do this:

Hot tip

You can enter the Start point as your current location. Tap once on this button to view your current location.

Beware

If you enter the name of a landmark you may also be shown other items that have the same name, such as businesses.

Hot tip

For some destinations, alternative routes will be displayed, depending on distance and traffic conditions. Tap once on the alternative route to select it. Directions for each route can be selected at the bottom of the window.

1 Tap once in the Search box at the bottom of the window in the Maps app

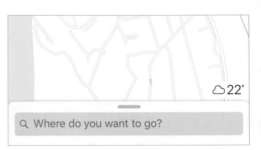

Q Where do you want to go?

2 Enter the destination (by default, this is from your current location)

3 Tap once on the **Directions** button. The route is shown on the map

Scone Robert Douglas Memori...
Real Estate · 2.7 mi

Directions
10 min drive

4 Tap once on these buttons at the bottom of the window to view the route for **Drive**, **Walk**, **Transit** or a taxi **Ride** using an appropriate app

To Scone Robert Douglas Mem...
From My Location

10 min
2.7 mi · South Street
Fastest route

GO

5 Tap once on the **Go** button to view step-by-step instructions on the map

6 The route is displayed, from your starting location. Audio instructions tell you the directions to be followed. You can use the volume buttons (on the side) to increase or decrease the sound. As you follow the route, the map and instructions are updated

The arrow in Step 6 points in the current direction of travel.

7 Swipe up from the bottom of the screen to access options for viewing items such as gas stations and food outlets on the route. These are displayed on the map, in relation to the current route being followed

Tap once on the **End** button and then the **End Route** button to stop following the current route.

Booking a Trip

Most major travel retailers have had their own websites for a number of years. They have now moved into the world of apps, and these can be used on your iPhone to book almost any type of vacation, from cruises to city breaks.

Several apps for the iPhone (and their associated websites) offer full travel services where they can deal with flights, hotels, insurance, car hire and excursions. These include:

- **Expedia**

- **Kayak**

- **Orbitz**

- **Travelocity**

These apps usually list special offers and last-minute deals on their Homepages and they offer options for booking flights, hotels, car hire and activities separately.

It is always worth searching different apps to get the best possible price. In some cases, it is cheapest to buy different elements of a vacation from different retailers, e.g. flights from one seller and accommodation from another.

Most travel apps have specific versions based on your geographical location. You will be directed to these by default.

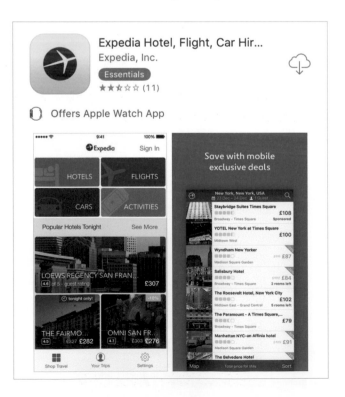

TripAdvisor

One of the best resources for travelers is TripAdvisor. Not only does the app provide a full range of opportunities for booking flights and hotels, it also has an extensive network of reviews from people who have visited the countries, hotels and restaurants on the site. These are independent, and usually very fair and honest. In a lot of cases, if there are issues with a hotel or restaurant, the proprietor posts a reply to explain what is being done to address any problems.

TripAdvisor has a certain sense of community, so post your own reviews once you have been places, to let others know about your experience.

Cruises

There are also apps dedicated specifically to cruises. One to look at is iCruise, which searches over a range of companies for your perfect cruise.

Booking Hotels

The internet is a perfect vehicle for finding good-value hotel rooms around the world. When hotels have spare capacity, this can quickly be relayed to associated websites and apps, where users can often benefit from cheap prices and special offers. There are plenty of apps that have details of thousands of hotels around the world, such as:

Trivago

An app that searches over one million hotels on more than 250 sites, to ensure you get the right hotel for the best price.

Hotels.com

A stylish app that enables you to enter search keywords into a Search box on the Home screen to find hotels based on destination, name or local landmarks.

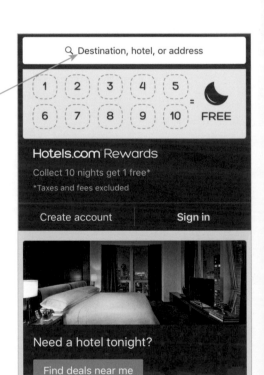

Booking.com

Another good, fully-featured hotel app that provides a comprehensive service and excellent prices.

LateRooms.com

An app that specializes in getting the best prices by dealing with rooms that are available at short notice. Some genuine bargains can be found here, for hotels of all categories.

Hot tip

Most hotel apps have reviews of all of the listed establishments. It is always worth reading these, as it gives you a view from the people who have actually been there.

Hot tip

Currency converters can also be downloaded from the App Store so that you can see how much your money is worth in different countries.

Finding Flights

Flying is a common part of modern life and although you do not have to book separate flights for a vacation (if it is part of a package), there are a number of apps for booking flights and also for following the progress of those in the air:

Skyscanner

This app can be used to find flights at airports around the world. Enter your details such as leaving airport, destination and dates of travel. The results show a range of available options, covering different price ranges and airlines.

Flight apps need to have an internet connection in order to show real-time flight information.

163

Flightradar24

If you like viewing the path of flights that are in the air, or need to check if flights are going to be delayed, this app provides this inflight information. Flights are shown according to flight number and airline.

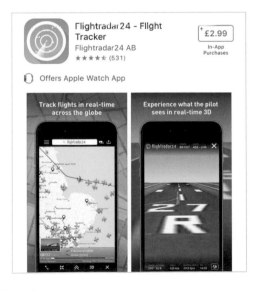

FlightAware Flight Tracker

Another app for tracking flights, showing arrivals and departures and also information about delays. It can track commercial flights worldwide.

Speaking Their Language

When you are traveling abroad it is always beneficial to learn some of the language of the country you are visiting. With your iPhone at hand this has become a whole lot easier, and there are a number of options:

Hot tip

There are also some keyboard translator apps in the App Store that can be used to translate items that you receive in any app. One to look at is **Keyboard plus (translator keyboard)**.

164

1 Translation apps that can be used to translate words, phrases and sentences in every language you probably need

2 Language apps that offer options in several languages

Some language apps are free, but they then charge for additional content, known as in-app purchases.

3 Specific language apps where you can fully get to grips with a new language

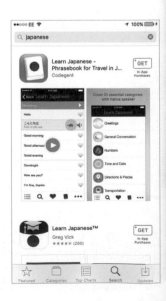

11 Camera and Photos

The iPhone 7 has a high-quality camera and the Photos app for viewing your photos.

The iPhone Camera

Because of its mobility and the quality of the screen, the iPhone is excellent for taking and displaying photos and videos. Photos can be captured directly using one of the two built-in cameras (one on the front and one on the back) and then viewed, edited and shared using the Photos app. To do this:

The camera on the back of the iPhone 7 is a 12 megapixel iSight one and is capable of capturing high-resolution photos and also high definition and 4K videos. The front-facing one is a 7 megapixel one and is excellent for video calls using FaceTime.

1. Tap once on the **Camera** app

2. Tap once on this button to capture a photo

3. Tap once on this button to swap between the front or back cameras on the iPhone

4. To take a quick photo, open the **Camera** app and press on either of the volume buttons

The iPhone 7 Plus has a dual-lens iSight camera, using a telephoto lens and a wide-angle one, for additional versatility when taking photos.

The iPhone cameras can be used for different formats:

1 Swipe left or right just above the shutter button, to access the different shooting options

2 Tap once on the **Square** button to capture photos at this ratio

3 Tap once on the **Video** button and press the red shutter button to take a video

Beware

When a video has been captured it is stored within the **Photos** app.

4 Tap once on the **Time-lapse** button and press the shutter button (which appears red with a ring around it) to create

a time-lapse image: the camera keeps taking photos periodically until you press the shutter button again

5 Tap once on the **Slo-Mo** button and press the red shutter button to take a slow-motion video

6 Tap once on the **Pano** button to create a panoramic image

7 Move the iPhone slowly to the right to create the panorama. Each photo will be taken automatically when the camera is in the correct position

Move iPhone continuously when taking a Panorama.

Don't forget

The HDR (High Dynamic Range) function can be used to take the same scene with different exposures, which are then combined into a single shot, with the different exposures merged together to give a better image.

Don't forget

When a filter effect has been selected, this button is displayed in the top right-hand corner of the camera window. It remains active until it is turned off. To do this, tap once on the button to access the filters and tap once on **None**.

...cont'd

Camera functions

The buttons at the top of the camera window can be used to create additional functionality.

1 Tap once on the **Flash** button to set it for **Auto**, **On** or **Off**

2 Tap once on the **Self-timer** button to set it for **Off**, **3s** or **10s**

3 Tap once on the **HDR** button to set it for **Auto**, **On** or **Off**

4 Tap once on this button to add a filter effect before you take a photo

Live Photos

One feature on the camera is the Live Photos functionality. This enables you to take what seems like a single photo, but it creates an animated photo, which is actually a short video clip. To take Live Photos:

1 Tap once on this button on the top toolbar until it turns yellow and **Live** appears

2 Take the photo as normal, making sure that it includes some movement

3 Press and hold on a Live Photo in the **Photos** app to view the animated effect

Camera Settings

iCloud sharing

Certain camera options can be applied within Settings. Several of these are to do with storing and sharing your photos via iCloud. To access these:

1 Tap once on the **Settings** app

2 Tap once on the **Photos & Camera** tab

3 Drag the **iCloud Photo Library** button to **On** to upload your whole iPhone photo library to the iCloud. You will then be able to access this from any other Apple devices that you have. Similarly, photos on your other Apple devices can also be uploaded to the iCloud and these will be available on your iPhone (requires other devices to be running iOS 8, or later, for mobile Apple devices or OS X Yosemite, or later, for desktop or laptop ones)

iCloud Photo Library	

Don't forget

Drag the **Grid** button in the Photos & Camera settings to **On** to place a grid over the screen when you are taking photos with the camera, if required. This can be used to help compose photos by placing subjects using the grid.

4 Drag the **Upload to My Photo Stream** button to **On** to enable all new photos and videos from your iPhone to be uploaded automatically to iCloud

Upload to My Photo Stream	

5 Drag the **iCloud Photo Sharing** button to **On** to allow you to create albums within the Photos app that can then be shared with other people via iCloud

iCloud Photo Sharing	

Viewing Photos

Once photos have been captured they can be viewed and organized in the Photos app. To do this:

Hot tip

Tap once on the magnifying glass icon at the top of the Years, Collections or Moments windows to search for photos.

1 Tap once on the **Photos** app

2 At the top level, all photos are displayed according to the years in which they were taken

3 Tap once within the **Years** window to view photos according to specific, more defined, timescales and locations. This is the **Collections** level. Tap once on the **Years** button to move back up one level

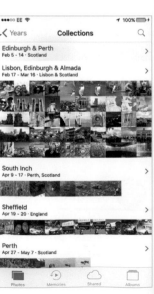

4 Tap once within the **Collections** window to drill down further into the photos, within the **Moments** window. Tap once on the **Collections** button to go back up one level

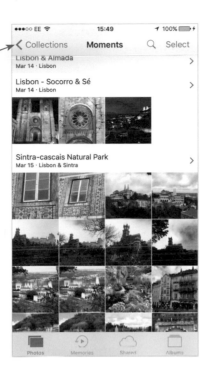

Moments are created according to the time at which the photos were added or taken: photos added at the same time will be displayed within the same Moment.

5 Tap once on a photo within the **Moments** window to view it at full size. Tap once here to go back up one level

Double-tap with one finger on an individual photo to zoom in on it. Double-tap with one finger again to zoom back out. To zoom in to a greater degree, swipe outwards with thumb and forefinger. To zoom back out, pinch inwards with thumb and forefinger.

6 Swipe left and right to move through all of the available full-size photos in a specific Moment

171

...cont'd

Viewing Memories

The Photos app also has a section where the best of your photos are selected and displayed automatically. To use this:

1 Tap once on the **Memories** button on the bottom toolbar

2 The Photos app automatically collates photos into groups of Memories, based on criteria such as location, people or **Best of Last 3 Months**. Tap once on a Memory to view the photos within it

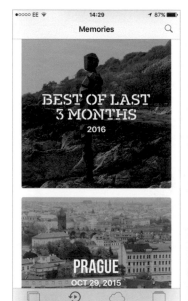

Hot tip

The **Memories** section is a great way to view the best of your photos from a trip or a vacation, without having to sort through them yourself.

3 The Photos app selects what it considers the best photos for each Memory and displays them on the page. Swipe down the page to view the photos. It also creates a movie (slideshow). Tap once here to view the movie

...cont'd

4 The Memories movie shows the photos in a variety of formats to give an attractive display

5 Tap once on a movie as it is playing to view the timeline at the bottom of the screen and also settings to customize the slideshow

Options for customizing a Memories movie include the style, which determines the title style and transitions between photos and the overall speed of the movie.

6 Swipe down to the bottom of the Memory in Step 3 to view a map with the locations of the photos and also related Memories, based on similar locations and people

Tap once on this button at the right-hand side of the panel in Step 5 to access more Settings for a movie, including editing the title, adding music and adding more photos.

Editing Photos

The Photos app has options to perform some basic photo-editing operations. To use these:

1 Open a photo at full-screen size and tap once on this button to access the editing tools, on the bottom toolbar

2 Tap once on the **Enhance** button to have auto-coloring editing applied to the photo

3 Tap once on the **Crop** button and drag the resizing handles to select an area of the photo that you want to keep and click **Done** to discard the rest

4 From the Crop section, tap once on the **Rotate** button to rotate the photo 90 degrees at a time, anti-clockwise

5 Tap once on the **Filters** button to select special effects to be applied to the photo

6 Tap once on the **Exposure** button to enable manual color editing for different options

Hot tip

If you reopen a photo that has been edited and closed, you have an option to **Revert** to its original state, before it was edited.

7 For each function, tap once on the **Done** button to save the photo with the selected changes

8 Tap once on the **Cancel** button to quit the editing process

Adding Albums

Albums can be used in the Photos app to store photos for different events or categories.

Photos can be selected in the same way as in Step 4 and used in other ways, too. For instance, they can be selected and then shared to other people, using the **Share** button or deleted, using the **Trash** button.

Tap once on the **Share** button on the bottom toolbar of the Photos app to create albums, which can then be shared with other people. Tap once on this button in the Shared section to create a new album for sharing.

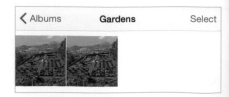

1 Open the **Photos** app and tap once on the **Albums** button on the bottom toolbar

Albums

2 Tap once on this button to create an album

3 Give the album a name and tap once on the **Save** button

New Album
Enter a name for this album.

Gardens

Cancel · Save

4 In the Moments section, tap once on the top **Select** button to select all the items in a Moment

< Collections · **Moments** · Done

12 March — Select

15 March — Select

5 Tap on any individual photos to deselect them, and then tap once on the **Done** button

< Collections · **Moments** · Done

12 March — Deselect

15 March — Deselect

6 The selected items are added to the album (they stay in their original location too)

< Albums · **Gardens** · Select

12 Practical Matters

This chapter looks at accessibility, security and finding an iPhone.

Accessibility Issues

The iPhone tries to cater to as wide a range of users as possible, including those who have difficulty with vision, hearing or physical and motor issues. There are a number of settings that can help with these areas. To access the range of Accessibility settings:

1 Tap once on the **Settings** app

2 Tap once on the **General** tab

3 Tap once on the **Accessibility** link Accessibility

4 The settings for **Vision**, **Interaction**, **Hearing**, **Media** and **Learning** are displayed here

You will have to scroll down the page to view the full range of Accessibility options.

178

Drag the **On/Off Labels** button to **On** to show the relevant icons on the On/Off buttons.

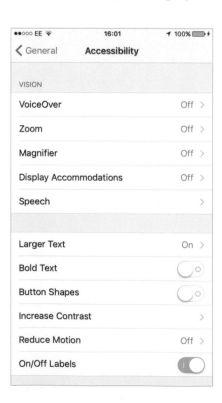

Accessibility screen listing:

VISION

VoiceOver	Off >
Zoom	Off >
Magnifier	Off >
Display Accommodations	Off >
Speech	>
Larger Text	On >
Bold Text	
Button Shapes	
Increase Contrast	>
Reduce Motion	Off >
On/Off Labels	

Vision settings

These can help anyone with impaired vision. There are options to hear items on the screen and also for making text easier to read:

1 Tap once on the **VoiceOver** link

VoiceOver	Off >

2 Drag this button to **On** to activate the VoiceOver function. This then enables items to be spoken when you tap on them

3 Select options for VoiceOver as required, such as speaking rate and pitch

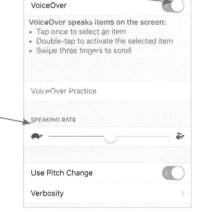

4 Tap once on an item to select it (indicated by the black outline) and have it read out. Double-tap to activate a selected item or perform an action

Beware

VoiceOver works with the pre-installed iPhone apps and some apps from the App Store, but not all of them.

Don't forget

Another useful Accessibility function is **AssistiveTouch**, within the **Interaction** section. This offers a range of options for accessing items via tapping on the screen, rather than having to use swiping with two, or more, fingers. Tap once on this icon to access the items within AssistiveTouch after it has been turned **On**.

...cont'd

Zoom settings

Although the iPhone 7 and iPhone 7 Plus screens are among the largest in the smartphone market, there are times when it can be beneficial to increase the size of the items that are being viewed. This can be done with the Zoom feature. To use this:

1 Access the

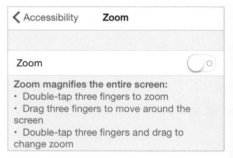

Accessibility section as shown on page 178 and tap once on the Zoom link

2 By default, the **Zoom** button is **Off**

Drag the **Show Controller** button to **On** in the Zoom settings to display a control button for the Zoom window. Tap once on the control button to view its menu of additional features, such as zooming in to greater or lesser amounts.

3 Drag the **Zoom** button to **On** to activate the Zoom window

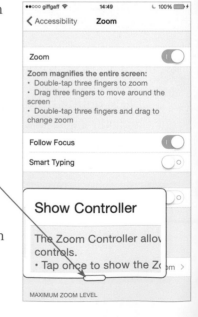

4 Drag on this button to move the Zoom window around the current screen. Drag with three fingers within the Zoom window to move the screen area within it

5 The Zoom window can also be used on the keyboard to increase the size of the keys. As in Step 4, drag with three fingers to move to other parts of the keyboard

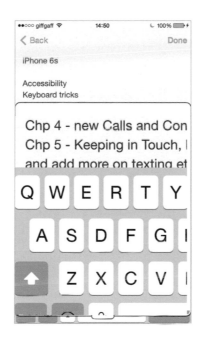

Text size can also be increased within the Accessibility settings. To do this:

1 Under the **Vision** section, tap once on the **Larger Text** link

Larger Text	Off >

2 Drag the **Larger Accessibility Sizes** button **On** to enable compatible apps to show larger text sizes

3 Drag this slider to set the text size

Beware

Not all apps support Dynamic Text for increasing text size, so the text in these apps will appear in their default sizes.

Setting Restrictions

Within the iPhone Settings app there are options for restricting types of content that can be viewed, and also actions that can be performed. These include:

- Turning off certain apps so that they cannot be used.

- Enabling changes to certain functions, so that only content that meets certain criteria can be accessed.

When setting restrictions, they can be locked so that no-one else can change them. To set and lock restrictions:

1 Tap once on the **Settings** app

It is a good idea to set up some restrictions on your iPhone if young children and grandchildren are going to have access to it.

2 Tap once on the **General** tab

 General

3 Tap once on the **Restrictions** link

Restrictions   Off >

4 The restrictions are grayed-out, i.e. they have not been enabled for use yet

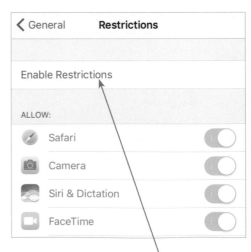

5 Tap once on the **Enable Restrictions** button

6 Type on the keypad to set a passcode for enabling and disabling restrictions (this is a four-digit code, as opposed to the six-digit one that can be used to lock and unlock the iPhone)

7 Re-enter the passcode

8 All of the Restrictions options become available. Drag these buttons **On** or **Off** to disable certain apps. If this is done they will no longer be visible on the Home screen

9 Tap once on the links under **Allowed Content** to specify restrictions for certain types of content, such as music, movies, books and apps

ALLOWED CONTENT:	
Ratings For	United States >
Music, Podcasts & News	Explicit >
Movies	All >
TV Shows	All >
Books	All >

You can set restrictions for criteria such as age groups or explicit content. However, if you do this for specific individuals, such as grandchildren, explain to them what you have done and why.

183

Location Services and **Find My iPhone** both have to be turned **On** to enable this service. This can be done in the Settings app (**Settings** > **Privacy** > **Location Services** > **Find iPhone** and under **Allow Location Access** tap once on **While Using the App**).

If you are using Family Sharing (see pages 58-63) you can use Find My iPhone to locate the devices of other Family Sharing members. This can be done from your online iCloud account, or with the Find My iPhone app.

Finding your iPhone

No-one likes to think the worst, but if your iPhone is lost or stolen, help is at hand. The Find My iPhone function (operated through the iCloud service) allows you to locate a lost iPhone and send a message and an alert to it. You can also remotely lock it or even wipe its contents. This gives added peace of mind, knowing that even if your iPhone is lost or stolen, its contents will not necessarily be compromised. To set up Find My iPhone:

1 Tap once on the **Settings** app

2 Tap once on the **iCloud** tab

3 Tap once on the **Find My iPhone** link (if it is showing **Off**. If it is **On** then Find My iPhone is already activated)

4 Drag the **Find My iPhone** button to **On** to be able to find your iPhone on a map

Finding a lost iPhone

Once you have set up Find My iPhone you can search for it through the iCloud service. To do this:

1 Log in to your iCloud account at **www.icloud.com**

2 Tap once on the **Find iPhone** button (you also have to sign in again with your Apple ID for this functionality)

3 Tap once on the **All Devices** button and select your iPhone. It is identified and its current location is displayed on the map

4 Tap once on the green circle to view details about when your iPhone was located

Click once on the **Erase iPhone** button to delete the iPhone's contents. This should be done as a last resort, if you think the contents may be compromised.

5 Tap once on the **Play Sound** button to send a sound alert to your iPhone

6 Tap once on the **Lost Mode** button to lock your iPhone

7 Add a phone number that will appear on the lost iPhone (optional) and click on the **Next** button. Add a message that will appear on the iPhone and click on the **Done** button. The iPhone can now only be unlocked with an existing passcode

If you have Apple Pay set up on your iPhone, this will be suspended if Lost Mode is enabled. It will be reactivated when the passcode is entered to unlock it and your Apple ID entered within Settings.

Avoiding Viruses

As far as security from viruses on the iPhone is concerned, there is good news and bad news:

Malware is short for malicious software, designed to harm your iPhone or access and distribute information from it.

- The good news is that, due to its architecture, most apps on the iPhone do not communicate with each other, unless specifically required to, such as the Mail and the Contacts apps. So, even if there were a virus, it would be difficult for it to infect the whole iPhone. Also, Apple performs rigorous tests on apps that are submitted to the App Store (although even this is not foolproof; see next bullet point).

- The bad news is that no computer system is immune from viruses and malware, and complacency is one of the biggest enemies of computer security. The iPhone's popularity means it is an attractive target for hackers and virus writers. There have been instances of photos in iCloud being accessed and hacked, but this was more to do with password security, or lack of, than viruses. Also, in September 2015 there was a malicious attack centered around the code used to create apps for the App Store. Although this was detected, some apps were affected before the virus was located and remedial action taken. This was known as the XcodeGhost attack and was a reminder of the need for extreme vigilance against viruses and for users to check in the media for information about any new attacks.

Apple also checks apps that are provided through the App Store, and this process is very robust. This does not mean that it is impossible for a virus to infect the iPhone, so keep an eye on the Apple website to see if there are any details about iPhone viruses.

Antivirus options

There are a few apps in the App Store that deal with antivirus issues, although not actually removing viruses. Some options to look at:

- **NowSecure Protect**. This free app checks your iPhone for malicious software that has been added.

- **McAfee** apps. The online security firm has a number of apps which cover issues such as privacy and passwords.

- **Norton** apps. Similar to McAfee, Norton offers a range of security apps for the iPhone.

Index